CliffsQuickReview™
French I

By Gail Stein

Hungry Minds™

Best-Selling Books • Digital Downloads • e-Books • Answer Networks • e-Newsletters • Branded Web Sites • e-Learning

Cleveland, OH • Indianapolis, IN • New York, NY

About the Author

Gail Stein, a French teacher for 30 years, has written numerous textbooks.

Publisher's Acknowledgments

Editorial

Project Editor: Tere Drenth

Acquisitions Editor: Roxane Cerda

Technical Editor: Simone Pilon

Editorial Administrator: Michelle Hacker

Production

Indexer: TECHBOOKS Production Services

Proofreader: Jennifer Mahern

Hungry Minds Indianapolis Production Services

CliffsQuickReview™ French I

Published by

Hungry Minds, Inc.

909 Third Avenue

New York, NY 10022

www.hungryminds.com

www.cliffsnotes.com

Library of Congress Control Number: 2001039071

ISBN: 0-7645-6379-3

Printed in the United States of America

10 9 8 7 6 5 4 3 2

1O/OT/QY/QR/IN

Distributed in the United States by Hungry Minds, Inc.

Distributed by CDG Books Canada Inc. for Canada; by Transworld Publishers Limited in the United Kingdom; by IDG Norge Books for Norway; by IDG Sweden Books for Sweden; by IDG Books Australia Publishing Corporation Pty. Ltd. for Australia and New Zealand; by TransQuest Publishers Pte Ltd. for Singapore, Malaysia, Thailand, Indonesia, and Hong Kong; by Gotop Information Inc. for Taiwan; by ICG Muse, Inc. for Japan; by Intersoft for South Africa; by Eyrolles for France; by International Thomson Publishing for Germany, Austria and Switzerland; by Distribuidora Cuspide for Argentina; by LR International for Brazil; by Galileo Libros for Chile; by Ediciones ZETA S.C.R. Ltda. for Peru; by WS Computer Publishing Corporation, Inc., for the Philippines; by Contemporanea de Ediciones for Venezuela; by Express Computer Distributors for the Caribbean and West Indies; by Micronesia Media Distributor, Inc. for Micronesia; by Chips Computadoras S.A. de C.V. for Mexico; by Editorial Norma de Panama S.A. for Panama; by American Bookshops for Finland.

For general information on Hungry Minds' products and services please contact our Customer Care department; within the U.S. at 800-762-2974, outside the U.S. at 317-572-3993 or fax 317-572-4002.

For sales inquiries and resellers information, including discounts, premium and bulk quantity sales, and foreign-language translations, please contact our Customer Care Department at 800-434-3422, fax 317-572-4002 or write to Hungry Minds, Inc., Attn: Customer Care Department, 10475 Crosspoint Boulevard, Indianapolis, IN 46256.

For information on licensing foreign or domestic rights, please contact our Sub-Rights Customer Care Department at 212-884-5000

For information on using Hungry Minds' products and services in the classroom or for ordering examination copies, please contact our Educational Sales Department at 800-434-2086 or fax 317-572-4005.

Please contact our Public Relations Department at 212-884-5163 for press review copies or 212-884-5000 for author interviews and other publicity information or fax 212-884-5400.

For authorization to photocopy items for corporate, personal, or educational use, please contact Copyright Clearance Center, 222 Rosewood Drive, Danvers, MA 01923, or fax 978-750-4470.

CQR Pocket Guide
French I

Essential Words and Phrases

The following chart lists the words and phrases you'll use most frequently when speaking French. Use it as a quick reference guide.

French	English
Bonjour.	Hello.
Au revoir.	Good-bye.
Je m'appelle	My name is . . . .
Comment vous appelez-vous?	What's your name?
Comment allez-vous?	How are you?
Pardon.	Excuse me.
Désolé(e).	I'm sorry.
Je me suis égaré(e).	I'm lost.
Où est . . .	Where is . . .
. . . l'arrêt de bus?	. . . the bus stop?
. . . la station de métro?	. . . the subway station?
. . . la gare?	. . . the train station?
. . . le commissariat de police?	. . . the police station?
. . . l'ambassade américaine?	. . . the American Embassy?
J'ai perdu . . .	I've lost . . .
. . . mon portefeuille.	. . . my wallet.
. . . mon passeport.	. . . my passport.
. . . mon argent.	. . . my money.
. . . ma carte de crédit.	. . . my credit card.
Aidez-moi, s'il vous plaît.	Help me, please.
Parlez plus lentement.	Speak more slowly.
Je ne vous comprends pas.	I don't understand you.
Comment dit-on . . . en français?	How do you say . . . in French?
Quelle heure est-il?	What time is it?
Parlez-vous anglais?	Do you speak English?

CQR Pocket Guide
French I

Important Signs

When you understand signs, you're less likely to endanger yourself or commit a *faux pas* (a mistake). Use the following guide to help you understand what the most common signs indicate.

French	English
À Louer	For Rent
Ascenseur	Elevator
À Vendre	For Sale
Dames	Ladies
Défense d'Entrer	Do Not Enter
Défense de Cracher	No Spitting
Défense de Fumer	No Smoking
Défense de Marcher sur l'Herbe	Don't Walk on the Grass
Eau Non Potable	Don't Drink the Water
Eau Potable	Fresh Water
École	School
Entrée Interdite	No Entrance
Entrée Libre	Free Admission
Fermé	Closed
Hommes	Men
Libre	Free/unoccupied
Ne Pas Toucher	Don't Touch
Non-fumeurs	Nonsmokers
Ouvert	Open
Poussez	Push
Renseignements	Information
Sens Unique	One Way
Soldes	Sales
Sortie	Exit
Tirez	Pull

Table of Contents

INTRODUCTION

Bonjour! Learning French is a fabulous way to expand your horizons in our rapidly growing multicultural world. Whether you want to use your language skills as a student, traveler, or businessperson, speaking French can open many doors for you when you least expect it.

CliffsQuickReview French I is just the tool you need to guide you through a quick, comprehensive review of the basics of French structure and vocabulary. The clear-cut, concise explanations and thematic lists of high-frequency words are handy means of recalling what you already know and enhancing your memory. You can even use this book to learn new information that you never covered in school.

Why You Need This Book

Can you answer yes to any of these questions?

- Do you need to review the fundamentals of French fast?

- Do you need a course supplement to the rules of elementary and intermediate French?

- Do you need a concise, comprehensive reference for French vocabulary and grammar?

If so, then *CliffsQuickReview French I* is for you!

How to Use This Book

You can use this book in any way that fits your personal style for study and review — you decide what works best for your needs. You can either read the book from cover to cover or just look for the information you want and put it back on the shelf for later. The following are just a few ways you can search for topics:

- Use the Pocket Guide to find essential information, such as a listing of the most important words and phrases you'll need and a guide to important French signs.

- Look for areas of interest in the book's Table of Contents or use the index to find specific topics.

- Flip through the book, looking for subject areas at the top of each page.

- Get a glimpse of what you'll gain from a chapter by reading through the Chapter Check-In at the beginning of each chapter.

- Use the Chapter Checkout at the end of each chapter to gauge your grasp of the important information you need to know.

- Test your knowledge more completely in the CQR Review and look for additional sources of information in the CQR Resource Center.

- Use the glossary to find key terms fast. This book defines new terms and concepts where they first appear in the chapter. If a word is bold-faced, you can find a more complete definition in the book's glossary.

- Use the Appendices for easy access to a list of common synonyms and antonyms, a thematic vocabulary list, and a list of the most common verbs and their conjugations.

- Flip through the book until you find what you're looking for — this book is organized to gradually build on key concepts.

Visit Our Web Site

A great resource, www.cliffsnotes.com, features review materials, valuable Internet links, quizzes, and more to enhance your learning. The site also features timely articles and tips, plus downloadable versions of many *CliffsNotes* books.

When you stop by our site, don't hesitate to share your thoughts about this book or any Hungry Minds product. Just click the Talk to Us button. We welcome your feedback!

Chapter 1

PRONOUNCING FRENCH

Chapter Check-In

❑ Using liaison and elision

❑ Understanding accents

❑ Pronouncing vowels

❑ Pronouncing nasal sounds

❑ Pronouncing consonants

French is a musical, romantic language, and its sounds need practice and a fair amount of attention. Although you can make yourself understood in French despite your own regional accent, use this chapter to help you sound as much like a native as possible.

Four areas need your undivided attention: accents, vowels, nasal sounds, and consonants, combined with the techniques of liaison and elision. The sounds of French vowels and nasals are quite different from the sounds you may be accustomed to in English; for that reason, vowels and nasals require some practice to obtain good results. Unlike English, French has accent marks that may or may not effect a change in pronunciation. In addition, many French consonants have the same pronunciation as those in English — only a few require additional concentration.

Keep in mind that each syllable in a French word has about equal stress, so by putting about the same emphasis on each syllable, you get the best results possible. Slightly stronger emphasis is placed on the last syllable of a group of words.

In addition, consider the following tips for better pronunciation:

■ Speak slowly and clearly.

■ Combine sounds and words for a more natural flow.

- Practice reading aloud authentic French materials.

- Listen to tapes and records to get a better feel for the sounds of the language.

- Don't be afraid to ham it up; that is, trying your best to sound like a native French speaker.

- Pay attention to accents and nasal sounds.

Liaison and Elision

Liaison refers to the linking of the final consonant of one word with the beginning vowel (a, e, i, o, u) or vowel sound (generally, h and y) to the following word, as in the following example: *vous imitez* (voo zee-mee-tay).

Note how pronunciation of the final *s* of *vous* takes on the sound of "z" and combines with the pronunciation of the beginning *i* of *imitez*.

Elision usually occurs when two vowel sounds are pronounced: one at the end of a word and the other at the beginning of the next word. Drop the final vowel of the first word and replace it with an apostrophe. The two words then simply slide together: *je + imite = j'imite* (zhee-meet).

Note how the final *e* (uh) sound of *je* (zhuh) is dropped.

Accents

An accent mark may change the sound of a letter, change the meaning of a word, replace a letter that existed in old French, or have no perceivable effect at all. Accents are used only on vowels and under the letter *c*.

- An **accent aigu** (´) is only used on an *e* (*é*) and produces the sound *ay*, as in "day." It may also replace an *s* from old French. When you see this letter, replace the *é* with an imaginary "s" to see if its meaning becomes more evident.

  étranger = stranger

- An **accent grave** (`) may be used on an *a* (*à*) or *u* (*ù*) where it causes no sound change, or on an *e* (*è*), producing the sound of *eh* as in the "e" in "get."

- An **accent circonflexe** (^) may be placed on any vowel but causes no perceptible sound change. It, too, often replaces an *s* from old French, which may give a clue to the meaning of the word.

forêt = forest

■ A **cédille** (̦) is placed under a *c* *(ç)*, to create a soft "s" sound before the letter *a, o,* or *u.*

ça (sah)

■ A **tréma** (¨) is placed on the second of two consecutive vowels to indicate that each vowel is pronounced independently.

Noël (noh-ehl)

Vowels

Some vowels in French have multiple pronunciations determined by specific linguistic rules, letter combinations, and/or accent marks, as shown in Table 1-1. You can always find exceptions, however, so when in doubt, consult a dictionary. In addition, expect sounds that are unfamiliar when vowels appear in combinations.

Table 1-1   Vowels and Their Sounds

Vowel	Sound
a, à, â	ah as in m**a**
e, final *er* and *ez, es* in some one-syllable words, some *ai* and *et* combinations	ay as in d**ay**
e in one syllable words or in the middle of a word followed by one consonant	uh as in th**e**
è, ê, and *e* (plus two consonants or a final pronounced consonant), *et, ei, ai*	eh as in g**et**
i, î, y, ui	i as in magaz**i**ne
ill or *il* when preceded by a vowel *o* (before *se*)	y as in **y**ou
o (last pronounced sound of word) *ô, au, eau*	o as in g**o**
o when followed by a pronounced consonant other than *s*	oh as in l**o**ve

(continued)

Table 1-1 *(continued)*

Vowel	Sound
ou, où, oû	oo as in b**oo**t
oy, oi	wah as in **w**atch
u, ù, û	no English equivalent – try saying **ew** with lips rounded.

Nasal Sounds

French nasal sounds occur when a vowel is followed by a single *n* or *m* in the same syllable, as shown in Table 1-2. You must use your nose (which should vibrate a bit) and your mouth to make these sounds.

Table 1-2   Nasal Sounds

Nasal	Sound
an, en (am, em)	like on with minor emphasis on n
in, ain (im, aim)	like an with minor emphasis on n
ien	like yan in **yan**kee with minor emphasis on n
oin	like wa in **wa**g
on (om)	like on in wr**on**g
un (um)	like un in **un**cle

Keep in mind that the following combinations do not require nasalized vowel sounds:

- vowel + *nn* or *mm: bonne* (pronounced like bun in English)
- vowel + *n* or vowel + *m: mine* (pronounced like mean in English)

Consonants

The French consonants in Table 1-3 are pronounced the same as they are in English: b, d, f, k, l, m, n, p, s, t, v, z. Most final French consonants remain unpronounced except for c, r, f, and l (think of the word **careful**). When in doubt, consult a good dictionary.

Table 1-3   Consonant Sounds

Consonant	Sound
c + a, o, u	c as in **c**ar
c + e, i	s as in **s**ent
ch	sh as in ma**ch**ine
g + a, o, u; gu + e, i, y	g as in **g**o
g + e, i; ge + a, o	zh as in mea**s**ure
gn	ny as in u**ni**on
j	zh as in mea**s**ure
h	always silent
q and qu	k as in **k**ind
r	no equivalent — the sound is gutteral and pronounced at the back of the throat as if gargling
s between two vowels and the s in -sion	z as in **z**ero
t in -tion	s as in **s**ea
th	t as in **t**ea
x (before vowel)	eg as in l**eg**
x (before consonant)	xc as in e**xc**el

Chapter Checkout

Q&A

Choose the best pronunciation for each word:

  1. *billet*

    a. bee-yay
    b. bee-yeh
    c. bee-leh
    d. bee-lay

2. *gagner*

   a. gag-nay
   b. gag-heh
   c. gah-nyay
   d. gah-nyeh

3. *théâtre*

   a. tay-ah-truh
   b. teh-yah-tray
   c. thay-ah-truh
   d. thuh-yah-truh

Answers: 1. b **2.** c **3.** a

Pronounce the Phrase

Pronounce the following sentences:

4. *Je m'appelle Jean.* (My name is John.)

5. *J'adore les sports.* (I adore sports.)

Answers: 4. zhuh mah-pehl zhahn (nasal). **5.** zhah-dohr lay spohr

Chapter 2
DAILY TOOLS

Chapter Check-In

- ❑ Expressing greetings, salutations, and goodbyes
- ❑ Using numbers
- ❑ Expressing dates
- ❑ Expressing time
- ❑ Expressing weather
- ❑ Using cognates
- ❑ Avoiding false friends

This chapter gives you the basics — some important but relatively simple expressions you need to communicate in person in French. Proper greetings, salutations, and goodbyes are extremely important when you meet a **francophone** (a French-speaking person). In addition, expressing numbers and being able to tell or ask about the time are essential tools in many circumstances. And being able to express the day, the month, the date, the season, or the weather is beneficial in many social conversations, especially when you're making plans.

Cognates are words that are the same or similar in both French and English. If you know your cognates, simply turn on your French accent and *voilà* — you're speaking French! **False friends,** on the other hand, are words whose meanings are deceptive, so you don't want to misuse them and make mistakes. This chapter shows you the differences.

Greetings and Salutations

In France, a formal approach is *de rigueur* (mandatory) if you want to converse with a person whom you don't know at all or very well. Don't commit a *faux pas* (mistake) by addressing someone informally before you have established a strong friendship or relationship. Start and end your conversations correctly by consulting Tables 2-1 and 2-2.

Note that *vous* expresses "you" in formal conversation, whereas *tu* expresses "you" in informal conversation. A more detailed explanation appears in Chapter 4.

Table 2-1   Formal Greetings and Goodbyes

Greeting/Goodbye in English	French
Hello.	*Bonjour.*
Good evening.	*Bonsoir.*
Mr.	*monsieur*
Mrs.	*madame*
Miss (Ms.)	*mademoiselle*
What's your name?	*Comment vous appelez-vous?*
My name is . . .	*Je m'appelle . . .*
I'm happy to meet you.	*Je suis heureux(se) de faire votre connaissance.*
I'd like you to meet . . .	*Je vous présente . . .*
How are you?	*Comment allez-vous?*
Very well.	*Très bien.*
Not bad.	*Pas mal.*
So so.	*Comme ci comme ça.*
Goodbye.	*Au revoir.*
Good night.	*Bonne nuit.*

As a sign of respect, older French women are generally referred to and addressed as *madame,* despite their marital status. Because *mademoiselle* is reserved for younger women, use *madame* when in doubt.

After sunset, *bonsoir* is used as a greeting. Use *bonne nuit* if you are about to retire for the night.

Table 2-2   Informal Greetings and Goodbyes

Greeting/Goodbye in English	French
Hi.	Salut.
What's your name?	Tu t'appelles comment?
My name is . . .	Je m'appelle . . .
Pleased to meet you.	Enchanté(e).
I'd like you to meet . . .	Je te présente . . .
Bye.	Salut.
How are you?	Ça va?
Fine.	Ça va.
How's it going?	Ça marche?
Fine.	Ça marche.
What's new?	Quoi de neuf?
Nothing.	Rien.
See you soon.	À bientôt.
See you later.	À tout à l'heure.
See you tomorrow.	À demain.

Numbers

The French write two numbers differently than Americans do: The number 1 has a little hook on top, which makes it look like a 7. So, to distinguish a 1 from a 7, a line is put through the 7, to look like this: 7 .

In numerals and decimals, the French use commas where Americans use periods, and vice versa:

English	French
4,000	4.000
.95	0,95
$16.75	$16,75

Cardinal numbers

Consult Table 2-3 for a list of French **cardinal numbers,** the numbers we use for counting: 1, 2, 3, 4, and so on.

Table 2-3 **Cardinal Numbers**

Number	French
0	*zéro*
1	*un*
2	*deux*
3	*trois*
4	*quatre*
5	*cinq*
6	*six*
7	*sept*
8	*huit*
9	*neuf*
10	*dix*
11	*onze*
12	*douze*
13	*treize*
14	*quatorze*
15	*quinze*
16	*seize*
17	*dix-sept*
18	*dix-huit*
19	*dix-neuf*
20	*vingt*
21	*vingt et un*
22	*vingt-deux*
30	*trente*
40	*quarante*
50	*cinquante*
60	*soixante*
70	*soixante-dix*
71	*soixante et onze*

Number	French
72	*soixante-douze*
73	*soixante-treize*
74	*soixante-quatorze*
75	*soixante-quinze*
76	*soixante-seize*
77	*soixante-dix-sept*
78	*soixante-dix-huit*
79	*soixante-dix-neuf*
80	*quatre-vingts*
81	*quatre-vingt-un*
82	*quatre-vingt-deux*
90	*quatre-vingt-dix*
91	*quatre-vingt-onze*
92	*quatre-vingt-douze*
100	*cent*
101	*cent un*
200	*deux cents*
201	*deux cent un*
1,000	*mille*
2,000	*deux mille*
1,000,000	*un million*
2,000,000	*deux millions*
1,000,000,000	*un milliard*
2,000,000,000	*deux milliards*

Note the following about cardinal numbers:

■ **The conjunction *et* (and) is used only for the numbers 21, 31, 41, 51, 61, and 71.** In all other compound numbers through 99, *et* is dropped, and a hyphen is used.

■ Before a feminine noun *un* becomes *une*.

> *vingt et un hommes* (21 men)
>
> *vingt et une femmes* (21 women)

■ To form 70 to 79, use *soixante* plus 10, 11, 12, and so on.

■ To form 90 to 99, use *quatre-vingt* plus 10, 11, 12, and so on.

■ For *quatre-vingts* (80) and the plural of *cent* (100) for any number above 199, drop the *s* before another number, but not before a noun.

> *quatre-vingt-quinze euros* (95 euros)
>
> *quatre-vingts euros* (80 euros)
>
> *deux cent cinquante dollars* (250 dollars)
>
> *deux cents dollars* (200 dollars)

■ *Un* is not used before *cent* (100) and *mille* (1,000).

> *cent hommes* (100 men)
>
> *mille femmes* (1,000 women)

■ *Mille* doesn't take *s* in the plural.

> *deux mille dollars* (2,000 dollars)

■ *Mille* becomes *mil* in dates.

> *J'ai mille neuf cent dollars.* (I have 1,900 dollars.)
>
> *Je suis né en mil neuf cents dix.* (I was born in 1910.)

■ To express numbers between 1,000 and 9,999, where it is more convenient, you can avoid using *mille* and simply use *cent*.

> *mille cent* or *onze cents* (1,100)
>
> *mille neuf cents* or *dix-neuf cents* (1,900)

■ The following words are used to express common arithmetic functions.

> + (plus) is *et*
>
> − (minus) is *moins*
>
> × (times) is *fois*

÷ (divided by) is *divisé par*

= (equals) is *font*

Nouns of number

Some numbers are used as collective nouns to express a round number, and some are followed by *de (d')* before another noun, as shown in Table 2-4.

Table 2–4   Nouns of Number

French Nouns of Number	English
une dizaine	about ten
une douzaine	a dozen
une quinzaine	about fifteen
une vingtaine	about twenty
une cinquantaine	about fifty
une centaine	about a hundred
un millier	about a thousand
un million	a million
un milliard	a billion
une centaine de femmes	about 100 women
deux centaines* de femmes	about 200 women
deux douzaines* d'œufs	two dozen eggs
des milliers* de jouets	thousands of toys
un million de dollars	a million dollars
deux millions* de dollars	two million dollars
sept milliards* d'hommes	seven billion men

*Note that you add *s* to these numbers in the plural.

Ordinal numbers

Ordinal numbers allow you to express the floors in a building or numbers in a series. Most ordinal numbers are formed by adding *-ième* to the cardinal number, as shown in Table 2-5.

Table 2-5 Ordinal Numbers

Ordinal	French Translation
1st	*premier* or *première*
2nd	*deuxième* or *second(e)*
3rd	*troisième*
4th	*quatrième*
5th	*cinquième*
6th	*sixième*
7th	*septième*
8th	*huitième*
9th	*neuvième*
10th	*dixième*
11th	*onzième*
12th	*douzième*
20th	*vingtième*
21st	*vingt et un(e)ième*
72nd	*soixante-douzième*
100th	*centième*

Note the following about ordinal numbers:

■ *Premier* and *première* are abbreviated as follows:

premier: 1er

première: 1re

■ **All others ordinals get a superscript *e*, as follows:**

dixième: 10^{e}

centième: 100^{e}

■ **Except for *premier* and *second*, ordinal numbers are formed by adding *-ième* to the cardinal number.** The silent *e* is dropped before *-ième*: *quatrième, onzième,* and so on.

la quatrième fois (the fourth time)

■ **A *u* is added in *cinquième*, and a *v* replaces the *f* in *neuvième*.**

> *le cinquième chapitre* (the fifth chapter)

■ **Ordinal numbers agree in number and gender with the nouns they descibe.** *Premier (première)* and *second (seconde)* and numbers using *unième (uneième)* are the only ordinal numbers that have a feminine form.

> *le premier garçon* (the first boy)
>
> *la première fille* (the first girl)
>
> *les premières années* (the first years)
>
> *les vingt et unièmes anniversaires* (21st birthdays)

■ *Premier* **is used only for the first in a series.** For 21 to 71, *unième* is added after the conjunction *et* to express first, and it must agree in number and gender with the noun it modifies.

> *le cinquante et unième match* (the 51st match)
>
> *la quarante et uneième année* (the 41st year)

■ *Second(e)* **is generally used in a series that goes no higher than two.**

■ **Use *le* or *la* before *huit/huitième* and *onze/onzième*.** No elision is necessary.

> *le huitième jour* (the 8th day)
>
> *le onze juillet* (July 11)

■ **In French, cardinal numbers precede ordinal numbers.**

> *les quatre premières personnes* (the first four people)

Days and Dates

In order to express the date, you first must know the days of the week and the months of the year in French. All months, days of the week, and seasons in French are masculine and are not capitalized unless they are used at the beginning of a sentence.

Days and months

French calendars start with Monday as the first day of the week. Keep this in mind when making appointments. Tables 2-6 and 2-7 give you the days of the week and the months of the year, respectively.

Table 2-6   Days of the Week

Day in English	French
Monday	*lundi*
Tuesday	*mardi*
Wednesday	*mercredi*
Thursday	*jeudi*
Friday	*vendredi*
Saturday	*samedi*
Sunday	*dimanche*

Table 2-7   Months of the Year

Month in English	French
January	*janvier*
February	*février*
March	*mars*
April	*avril*
May	*mai*
June	*juin*
July	*juillet*
August	*août*
September	*septembre*
October	*octobre*
November	*novembre*
December	*décembre*

Dates

Dates in French may be expressed in several ways, as follows. Notice that *le* is optional or may be used in one of two places: *(le)* + day + *(le)* cardinal number + month + year. July 11, 2002 may expressed in any of the following ways:

■   *lundi onze juillet 2002*

- *lundi le onze juillet 2002*
- *le lundi onze juillet 2002*

Note the following when expressing a date:

- **The first of each month is expressed by** *premier,* **but** *premier* **is the only ordinal number used.** Cardinal numbers are used for all other days.

    le premier avril (April 1st)

    le deux mars (March 2nd)

    le neuf juin (June 9th)

- **Years are usually expressed in hundreds, just like in English.**

    dix-neuf cent quatre-vingt-dix-neuf (1999)

    mil neuf cent quatre-vingt-dix-neuf (1999)

    deux mille (2000)

- **When writing the date in numbers, the French follow the sequence day + month + year, just as they do in speaking.**

    le 3 mai 2002 (May 3, 2002) which is expressed as *3/5/02* (5/3/02)

- **The word for year,** *an,* **is used with ordinal numbers (1, 2, 3, and so on) unless an adjective is used to describe the word "year," in which case the word** *année* **is used to express year. Sometimes, either word is acceptable.**

    un an (a year)

    une année (a year)

    six bonnes années (six good years)

    quelques années (some years)

    l'an dernier (last year)

    l'année dernière (last year)

- **To express "on" a certain day, the French use the definite article** *le,* **explained in more detail in Chapter 3.**

    Le lundi je vais en ville. (On Monday[s], I go downtown.)

- **The English words "on" and "of" are not expressed in French dates.**

  Il arrive le quatorze septembre. (He's arriving on September 14th).

  Nous partons le quinze avril. (We're leaving on the 15th of April.)

- **Use the preposition *en* to express "in" with months.**

  Je voyage en juillet. (I travel in July.)

- **Use the following questions to receive or give information pertaining to today's day or date.** You can also use the same questions to receive or give information about the day or date of an event by changing *aujourd'hui* (today) to the day, date, or event in question.

  Quel jour est-ce aujourd'hui? What day is today? *C'est aujourd'hui . . .* (Today is . . .)

  Quel jour sommes-nous aujourd'hui? (What day is today?) *Nous sommes aujourd'hui . . .* (Today is . . .)

  Quelle est la date d'aujourd'hui? (What's today's date?) *C'est aujourd'hui . . .* (Today is . . .)

The words and expressions in Table 2-8 may prove invaluable to you when you need information about a period of time.

Table 2-8   Periods of Time

Time Period in English	French
a day	un jour
a week	une semaine
a month	un mois
a year	un an
a year	une année
in	dans/en
ago	il y a
per	par
during	pendant

Time Period in English	French
next	prochain(e)
last	dernier (dernière)
last	passé(e)
eve	la veille
day before yesterday	avant-hier
yesterday	hier
today	aujourd'hui
tomorrow	demain
day after tomorrow	après-demain
next day	le lendemain
a week from today	d'aujourd'hui en huit
two weeks from tomorrow	de demain en quinze

Time

Consider the following questions and answers you'll need to be on top of the time.

- *Quelle heure est-il?* (What time is it?) *Il est . . .* (It is . . .)
- *À quelle heure . . . ?* (At what time . . . ?) *À . . .* (At . . .)

Consult Table 2-9 to tell time correctly in French.

Table 2-9   Telling Time

Time	French Spelling
1:00	une heure
2:05	deux heures cinq
3:10	trois heures dix
4:15	quatre heures et quart
5:20	cinq heures vingt
6:25	six heures vingt-cinq

(continued)

Table 2-9 *(continued)*

Time	French Spelling
7:30	*sept heures et demie*
7:35	*huit heures moins vingt-cinq*
8:40	*neuf heures moins vingt*
9:45	*dix heures moins le quart*
10:50	*onze heures moins dix*
11:55	*midi moins cinq*
midnight	*minuit*
noon	*midi*

To express and understand time properly remember the following:

■ To express time after the hour, the number of minutes is added. *Et* (and) is used only with *quart* (quarter) and *demi(e)* (half).

■ *Moins* (less, minus) is used to express time before the hour.

■ *Moins le* is used before *quart* to express 15 minutes before the hour.

■ Because *midi* (noon) and *minuit* (midnight) are masculine, to say half past, use *et demi*, as in the following: *J'arrive à midi et demi.* (I'm arriving at half past noon.)

■ In public announcements, such as timetables, the official twenty-four-hour system is commonly used, with midnight as the zero hour:

16 h is 4:00 p.m.

21 h 45 is 9:45 p.m.

Seasons

At times, you may want to discuss what you do in the seasons.

■ *l'été* (summer)

■ *l'automne* (fall, autumn)

■ *l'hiver* (winter)

■ *le printemps* (spring)

To inquire and receive information about the season, use the following: *Quelle saison est-ce?* (What's the season?) *C'est . . .* (It's . . .)

The preposition *en* is used to express "in" with all the seasons, except with *printemps*, when the contraction *au (à + le)* is used:

- *en été* (in the summer)

- *en automne* (in the fall)

- *en hiver* (in the winter)

- *au printemps* (in the spring)

Weather

As you watch television, listen to the radio, or read the newspaper, you may see *la météo* (the forecast). Consult Table 2-10 for common weather expressions.

Table 2-10   Weather Conditions

French	*English Phrase*
Quel temps fait-il?	What's the weather?
Il fait beau.	It's beautiful.
Il fait chaud.	It's hot.
Il fait du soleil.	It's sunny.
Il fait mauvais.	It's nasty (bad).
Il fait froid.	It's cold.
Il fait frais.	It's cool.
Il fait du vent.	It's windy.
Il fait des éclairs.	It's lightning.
Il fait du tonnerre.	It's thundering.
Il fait du brouillard. Il y a du brouillard.	It's foggy.
Il fait humide. Il y a de l'humidité.	It's humid.
Il y a des nuages. Le ciel est nuageux.	It's cloudy.
Le ciel est couvert.	It's overcast.

(continued)

Table 2-10 *(continued)*

French	English Phrase
Il pleut.	It's raining.
Il pleut à verse.	It's pouring.
Il neige.	It's snowing.
Il y a des rafales.	There are gusts of wind.
Il y a de la grêle.	There's hail.
Il y a des giboulées.	There are sudden showers.

The following additional terms in Table 2-11 will help you interpret forecasts as you hear or see them.

Table 2-11   Terms Used in Forecasts

French Forecast	English
averses	showers (heavy rain)
bruines	drizzle
brumeux	hazy, foggy
ciel clair	clear sky
faible	weak
fort	strong
fraîcheur	chilly
modéré	moderate
orages	storms/rain
tempête	storm/snow
verglas	sleet

Keep in mind that the Centigrade (Celsius) thermometer is used in French-speaking countries.

■ To convert Fahrenheit to Centigrade, subract 32 from the Fahrenheit temperature and multiply the remaining number by ⅝. This will give you the temperature in degrees Centigrade.

■ To convert Centigrade to Fahrenheit, multiply the Centigrade temperature by ⅘ and add 32. This will give you the temperature in degrees Fahrenheit.

Use the thermometer in Figure 2-1 as a quick weather reference guide. To ask and receive answers about the temperature, use the phrases in Table 2-12.

Figure 2-1 Centigrade and Fahrenheit.

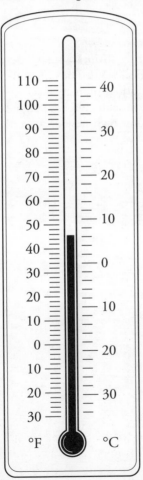

Table 2-12   Phrases Regarding Temperature

English Phrase	French
What's the temperature?	*Quelle est la température?* or *Quelle température fait-il?*
It's 5 below.	*Il fait moins cinq.*
It's zero.	*Il fait zéro.*
It's 70 degrees.	*Il fait soixante-dix.*

Cognates

A cognate is a word whose meaning is blatantly obvious because it exactly, or very closely, resembles an equivalent English word. The only difference between the two words lies in their pronunciation. In many instances, you can immediately recognize French words because the English language has appropriated them. Here, for example, are some high-frequency words you should find quite useful:

Words that are exactly the same:

- *adorable*
- *boutique*
- *bureau*
- *certain*
- *chef*
- *client*
- *content*
- *date*
- *minute* (time)
- *note*
- *permanent*
- *photo*
- *possible*
- *route* (road)

- *sandwich*
- *service*
- *soda*
- *variable*

Similar words are as follows:

- *adresse*
- *américain*
- *banque*
- *bleu*
- *cinéma*
- *confortable*
- *dictionnaire*
- *difficile*
- *docteur*
- *famille*
- *nécessaire*
- *occupé*
- *papier*
- *personne*
- *pharmacie*
- *supermarché*
- *téléphone*
- *télévision*

False Friends

False friends are words that are spelled the same or almost the same in both French and English but have entirely different meanings and can be different parts of speech. The most common ones to watch out for are in Table 2-13.

Table 2-13   False Friends

French	English
attendre	to wait (for)
comment	how
figure	face
librairie	bookstore
occasion	opportunity
pain	bread
rester	to remain
sale	dirty
travail	work

Chapter Checkout

Short Answer

Give the date, season, and general weather in your area for the following days:

Sample responses: 1. *C'est lundi le vingt-cinq décembre. C'est l'hiver. Il fait froid.* **2.** *C'est vendredi le quatre juillet. C'est l'été. Il fait chaud.* **3.** *C'est mercredi le neuf avril. C'est le printemps. Il fait du soleil.* **4.** *C'est jeudi le vingt novembre. C'est l'automne. Il fait frais.*

Fill in the Blank

Fill in the correct numbers and times from this ad in French:

CINÉMA CLUNY-PALACE

71 bd St Germain 5
(01)43 54 17 76

présente: **CHOCOLAT**

11h30   13h45   16h   18h15

1. _____ bd St Germain _____

2. (_____) _____ _____ _____ _____

3. 11h30 _____

4. 13h45 _____

5. 16h _____

Answers: 1. *soixante et onze, cinquième* **2.** *un, quarante-trois, cinquante-quatre, dix-sept, soixante-seize* **3.** *onze heures et demie* **4.** *deux heures moins le quart* **5.** *quatre heures*

Chapter 3
ARTICLES

Articles are small words that are generally classified as adjectives. They indicate that a noun or noun substitute will follow. French articles are singular or plural, depending upon whether the noun that follows is singular or plural. French singular articles vary depending upon whether the following noun is masculine or feminine, or whether it starts with a vowel or consonant. See Chapter 4 for more on French nouns.

Four French **definite articles** express the English word "the"; three French **indefinite articles** express "a," "an," and "one"; five **partitive articles** express "some" or "any"; and four **demonstrative adjectives** express "this," "that," "these," and "those."

Definite Articles

The **definite article,** which expresses the English word "the," indicates a specific person or thing: the family, for example. The masculine, feminine, singular, and plural forms are shown in Table 3-1.

For words beginning with a vowel or vowel sound (y and **unaspirated** h; that is, no puff of air is emitted when pronouncing the word — aspirated h is generally indicated in dictionaries by an * or another symbol), the singular definite articles *le* and *la* become *l'*. The masculine or feminine **gender** of the noun, so easily recognizable when *le* (masculine) or *la* (feminine) is used, becomes a problem when the noun that follows requires the use of *l'*, which represents either gender nouns before a vowel.

All plural nouns require the one plural definite article *(les)*, so you cannot determine the gender of plural nouns by the article.

Table 3-1   Definite Articles

	Masculine	*Feminine*
Singular	*le* or *l'*	*la* or *l'*
	le garçon (the boy)	*la fille* (the girl)
	l'homme (the man)	*l'actrice* (the actress)
Plural	*les*	*les*
	les garçons (the boys)	*les filles* (the girls)
	les hommes (the men)	*les actrices* (the actresses)

Use the definite article as follows:

- **With nouns in a general or abstract sense**

    J'adore les chiens. (I love dogs.)

- **With names of languages, except directly after *parler*, *en*, and *de***

    Le français est facile. (French is easy.)

    J'adore le français. (I love French.)

    But:

    Je parle français. (I speak French.)

    C'est en français. (It's in French.)

    une classe de français (a French class)

- **With parts of the body when the possessor is clear**

    Ouvre les yeux. (Open your eyes.)

- **With titles of rank or profession, except when addressing the person**

    le docteur Jean (Dr. John)

But:

> *Bonjour, docteur Jean.* (Hello, Dr. John.)

■ **With days of the week in a plural sense**

> *Le lundi je travaille.* (On Mondays, I work.)

■ **With seasons and colors, except after *au* or *en***

> *Tu aimes l'hiver?* (Do you like the winter?)
> *Il préfère le bleu.* (He prefers blue.)

But:

> *Au printemps il pleut.* (It rains in the spring.)
> *Je peins la maison en blanc.* (I'm painting the house white.)

■ **With dates**

> *C'est le dix août.* (It's August 10.)

■ **With most geographical names of countries and continents**

> *La France est super.* (France is super.)

■ **To express a, an, or per with weights and measures**

> *Il paie six dollars la douzaine.* (He pays $6 per dozen.)

■ **With common expressions of time or place**

> *le soir* (in the evening)
> *la semaine prochaine* (next week)
> *à la maison* (at home)

Indefinite Articles

Indefinite articles, shown in Table 3-2, refer to persons and objects not specifically identified: a girl, an apple, or some boys. Use different indefinate articles based on whether the noun that follows is masculine, feminine, singular, or plural.

The *e* from the indefinite article *une* is never dropped. This final *e* does, however, change the sound of the word *un,* which is nasalized, to *une,* which is not nasalized.

Table 3-2   Indefinite Articles

	Masculine	*Feminine*
Singular	*un*	*une*
	un garçon (a boy)	*une fille* (a girl)
	un ami (a friend)	*une amie* (a friend)
Plural	*des*	*des*
	des garçons (boys or some boys)	*des filles* (girls or some girls)
	des amis (friends or some friends)	*des amies* (friends or some friends)

Omit the indefinite article in the following cases:

■ **After the verbs *être* (to be) and *devenir* (to become) that come before the names of professions, except after *c'est* or when the noun is modified by an adjective**

> *Anne est docteur.* (Anne is a doctor.)

> *Luc devient avocat.* (Luc is becoming a lawyer.)

But:

> *C'est une actrice.* (She's an actress.)

> *C'est un dentiste.* (He's a dentist.)

> *M. Leconte est un patron populaire.* (Mr. Leconte is a popular boss.)

■ **After the exclamatory adjective *quel (quelle, quels, quelles)***

> *Quel garçon curieux!* (What a curious boy!)

> *Quelles maisons luxueuses!* (What luxurious houses!)

■ **Before the numbers *cent* (100) and *mille* (1,000)**

> *cent enfants* (one hundred children)

> *mille dollars* (one thousand dollars)

Partitive Articles

Use the **partitive article,** which expresses that you want part of a whole (some or any), to ask for an **indefinite quantity** (something that is not being counted). Before a noun, the partitive is generally expressed by *de* + the definite article. Note that *de* + *le* contract to become *du*, and *de* + *les* contract to become *des*, as shown in Table 3-3.

Table 3-3   Partitive Articles

Article	Used Before	Example
du	masculine singular nouns beginning with a consonant	*du temps* (some time)
de la	feminine singular nouns beginning with a consonant	*de la glace* (some ice cream)
de l'	any singular noun beginning with a vowel	*de l'argent* (some money)
des	any plural noun	*des gens* (some people)

Note the following about the use of the partitive article:

■ **Although the partitive "some" or "any" may be omitted in English, it may not be omitted in French and must be repeated before each noun.**

   Il prend des céréales et du lait. (He's having cereal and milk.)

■ **In a negative sentence, the partitive "some" or "any" is expressed by *de* or *d'* without the article.**

   Je ne mange jamais de fruits. (I never eat any fruits.)

   Je n'ai pas d'oranges. (I don't have any oranges.)

■ **Before a singular adjective preceding a singular noun, the partitive is expressed with or without the article.**

   C'est de (du) bon gâteau. (That's good cake.)

■ **Before a plural adjective preceding a plural noun, the partitive is expressed by *de* alone.**

   Ce sont de bons élèves. (They are good students.)

■ Certain nouns (see Chapter 4) and adverbs (see Chapter 11) of quantity are followed by the partitive article *de* (*d'* before a vowel).

Nouns	*Adverbs*
un boîte de (a box, can of)	*assez de* (enough)
un bol de (a bowl of)	*beaucoup de* (many, much, a lot of)
une tasse de (a cup of)	*peu de* (few, a little)
un verre de (a glass of)	*trop de* (too many, much)

Donnez-moi une tasse de café. (Give me a cup of coffee.)

Il a beaucoup d'amis. (He has a lot of friends.)

■ The following nouns and adverbs of quantity are followed by *de* + definite article (see Chapter 11 for more detail):

la plupart (most)

bien (a good many)

la majorité (the majority)

la plus grande partie (the majority)

La plupart des gens aiment ce film. (Most people like this movie.)

■ The adjectives *plusieurs* (several) and *quelques* (some) modify the noun directly.

J'adore plusieurs légumes. (I like several vegetables.)

Il achète quelques livres. (He is buying some books.)

■ The partitive is not used with *sans* (without) and *ne . . . ni . . . ni* (neither . . . nor).

Elle prendra du thé sans citron. (She'll take tea without lemon.)

Il ne boit ni café ni thé. (He doesn't drink coffee or tea.)

Definite Article Versus Partitive Article

Although the definite article *(le, la, l', les)* is used with nouns in a general sense, the partitive is used to express some or part of something:

- *J'adore le chocolat.* (I love chocolate.)

- *Donne-moi du chocolat.* (Give me some chocolate.)

Although you use *un* or *une* when speaking about one portion or serving, you use an adverb or noun of quantity or the partitive to express amounts:

- *Un chocolat chaud, s'il vous plaît.* (A hot chocolate, please.)

- *Un bol de chocolat, s'il vous plaît.* (A mug of hot chocolate, please.)

- *Du chocolat chaud, s'il vous plaît.* (Some hot chocolate, please.)

Demonstrative Adjectives

Demonstrative adjectives, shown in Table 3-4, precede and agree in number (singular or plural) and gender (masculine or feminine) with the nouns they modify. **Demonstrative adjectives** indicate or point out the person, place, or thing referred to. Singular demonstrative adjectives can mean either "this" or "that." Plural demonstrative adjectives can mean either "these" or "those."

Table 3-4   Demonstrative Adjectives

	Masculine	*Feminine*
Singular	*ce (cet)*	*cette*
	J'adore ce livre. (I love this book.)	*Cette robe est belle.* (That dress is beautiful.)
Plural	*ces*	*ces*
	J'achète ces livres. (I'm buying these books.)	*Ces filles sont amies.* (Those girls are friends.)

Note the following about demonstrative adjectives:

- **The masculine singular demonstrative adjective *cet* is used before a masculine singular noun that begins with a vowel or vowel sound to prevent a clash of vowel sounds.** When speaking, link the final *t* of *cet* with the vowel that follows.

    cet hotel (this/that hotel)

But:

> *cette actrice* (this/that actress)

■ **Repeat the demonstrative adjective before each noun.**

> *cet appartement et cette maison* (this apartment and that house)
>
> *ces hommes et ces femmes* (these men and women or these men and those women)

■ **If you must distinguish between this and that or these and those, for clarity, emphasis, comparison, or contrast, add the tags *ci* (from the word *ici,* which means "here") to mean this and these, and *là* (from the word *là,* which means "there") to mean that and those, to the nouns being compared.** They are attached with a hyphen, as follows:

> *cette fille-ci et ce garçon-là* (this girl and that boy)

Chapter Checkout

Fill in the Blank

Select the correct article to complete the sentence:

1. *J'aime* _____ *poulet.* (I like chicken.)

  a. *du*
  b. *le*
  c. *un*

2. *Donne-moi* _____ *argent, s'il te plaît.* (Please give me some money.)

  a. *de l'*
  b. *l'*
  c. *un*

3. *Je n'ai pas* _____ *frères.* (I don't have any brothers.)

  a. *du*
  b. *des*
  c. *de*

4. *La plupart* _____ *gens sont généreux.* (Most people are generous.)

  a. *des*

  b. *de la*

  c. *de*

5. *J'adore* _____ *actrice.* (I love that actress.)

  a. *cette*

  b. *ces*

  c. *cet*

Answers: 1. b **2.** a **3.** c **4.** a **5.** a

Chapter 4

NOUNS

In order to properly speak and write French (as well as other romance languages), many elements in a sentence must agree with the masculine or feminine noun to which you are referring. The gender of nouns, therefore, is important when constructing sentences.

To refer to more than one noun, you must be able to form plurals and nouns. While some plurals follow certain rules, other categories of nouns have irregular plurals that you must memorize.

The Gender of Nouns

A **noun** is a word used to name a person, place, thing, idea, or quality. In a bilingual dictionary, nouns may be designated by an *n.* (noun) or an *s.* (substantive, a word that stands for noun). Bilingual dictionaries, as well as this book, also use *m.* for masculine and *f.* for feminine. If you see *m./f.,* the noun may be either gender depending upon the person or thing to which you are referring.

Like English, all French nouns have a number: singular (one), as in *la famille* (the family), or plural (more than one), as in *les enfants* (the children). Unlike English, however, all French nouns also have a gender: masculine or feminine. In some instances, the gender of the noun is apparent: *Un garçon* (a boy) is masculine, whereas *une fille* (a girl) is feminine. In other cases, the gender of a noun is not at all obvious and defies all rules of common sense or logic: *Une chemise* (a man-tailored shirt) is feminine, while *un jupon* (a slip) is masculine.

No explanations are readily available to explain why French nouns have a certain gender or how the gender of any noun was originally determined, so you cannot rely on a rule to guide you; however, certain endings do generally indicate a feminine or masculine noun. For the most part, though, the gender of nouns must be memorized — through repetition, you can likely commit them to memory.

Obvious masculine and feminine nouns

Nouns that refer to males are always masculine and their female counterparts are always feminine, as shown in Table 4-1.

Table 4-1   Obvious Masculine or Feminine Nouns

Obvious Masculine Nouns	Obvious Feminine Nouns
fils (son)	*fille* (daughter)
garçon (boy)	*fille* (girl)
grand-père (grandfather)	*grand-mère* (grandmother)
homme (man)	*femme* (woman)
neveu (nephew)	*nièce* (niece)
oncle (uncle)	*tante* (aunt)
père (father)	*mère* (mother)
prince (prince)	*princesse* (princess)
roi (king)	*reine* (queen)

Nouns that give you a hint

In some cases, the gender of a noun can be determined by its ending, as shown in Table 4-2. Exceptions are the feminine words *page* (page of a book) and *plage* (beach) that end in *-age* and the feminine words *eau* (water) and *peau* (skin) that end in *-eau*.

Table 4-2   Endings That Determine Gender

Masculine Ending	Example	Feminine Ending	Example
-acle	*spectacle* (spectacle)	*-ade*	*orangeade* (orangeade)
-age	*village* (village)	*-ale*	*capitale* (capital)

Masculine Ending	Example	Feminine Ending	Example
-al	*journal* (newspaper)	-ance	*chance* (chance, luck)
-eau	*bureau* (office)	-ence	*agence* (agency)
-et	*cabinet* (office)	-ette	*raquette* (racket)
-ier	*papier* (paper)	-ie	*magie* (magic)
-isme	*cyclisme* (cycling)	-ique	*musique* (music)
-ment	*changement* (change)	-oire	*victoire* (victory)
		-sion	*version* (version)
		-tion	*nation* (nation)
		-ure	*coiffure* (hair style)

Nouns that change gender

Consider the following nouns, which can be either masculine or feminine, depending upon to whom you are referring. Make sure to use the proper article (*le, l', un* for masculine) or (*la, l', une* for feminine) before the noun. Articles are discussed in Chapter 3.

- *artiste* (artist)
- *camarade* (friend)
- *collègue* (colleague)
- *concierge* (superintendent)
- *élève* (student)
- *enfant* (child)
- *malade* (patient)
- *secrétaire* (secretary)
- *touriste* (tourist)

Some nouns can be easily changed from one gender to another by adding an *e* to the masculine form to get the feminine form, as shown in Table 4-3. Keep in mind that adding an *e* to a final consonant necessitates pronouncing that final consonant sound.

Table 4-3   Changing Genders

Masculine Ending	Feminine Ending	English
ami	amie	friend
avocat	avocate	lawyer
client	cliente	client
cousin	cousine	cousin
employé	employée	employee
étudiant	étudiante	student
Français	Française	French person
voisin	voisine	neighbor

Some masculine noun endings (usually referring to professions) have a corresponding feminine ending, as indicated in Table 4-4, that is used when the professional is female. The masculine *-an*, *-ien*, and *-on* endings are nasalized when pronounced, whereas the feminine counterparts are not.

Table 4-4   Special Feminine Endings

Masculine Ending	Feminine Ending	Example	English
-an	-anne	paysan(ne)	peasant
-el	-elle	contractuel(le)	meter reader
-er	-ère	boucher (bouchère)	butcher
-eur	-euse	vendeur (vendeuse)	sales clerk
-ien	-ienne	musicien(ne)	musician
-on	-onne	patron(ne)	boss
-teur	-trice	acteur (actrice)	actor

Some nouns have different meanings depending upon whether they are used in a masculine or feminine sense. Consult Table 4-5 to use these words correctly.

Table 4-5   Meanings Determined by Gender

Masculine Words	Feminine Words
le critique (critic)	*la critique* (criticism)
le livre (book)	*la livre* (pound)
le mémoire (report)	*la mémoire* (memory)
le mode (method)	*la mode* (fashion)
le poste (job)	*la poste* (post office)
le tour (tour)	*la tour* (tower)
le vase (vase)	*la vase* (mud)

Nouns with gender that must be memorized

Some high-frequency words are always masculine or feminine, despite the gender of the person referred to. Don't be tempted to select the article you use based on the gender of the person about whom you are speaking:

- *un agent de police* (a police officer)
- *un bébé* (a baby)
- *un chef* (a chef, a leader, a head)
- *un docteur* (a doctor)
- *un écrivain* (a writer)
- *un ingénieur* (an engineer)
- *un mannequin* (a model)
- *un médecin* (a doctor)
- *un peintre* (a painter)
- *un pompier* (a firefighter)
- *un professeur* (a teacher)
- *une connaissance* (an acquaintance)
- *une personne* (a person)
- *une star* (a star)
- *une vedette* (a star)
- *une victime* (a victim)

The Plural of Nouns

Just like in English, when a French noun refers to more than one person, place, thing, idea, or quality, it must be made plural. Keep in mind that when changing the noun to the plural, its respective article must also change to the plural.

Using a plural article before a noun does not enable you to determine the gender of any noun. The only information provided by plural articles is that the speaker is referring to more than one noun. You can learn noun genders only by studying each noun with its singular article, as discussed in the preceding section and in Chapter 3.

Most nouns in French are made plural by simply adding an unpronounced *s* to the singular form:

- *la famille* becomes *les familles*
- *un élève* becomes *des élèves*

The letters *s*, *x*, and *z* are all used to make plurals in French. If a singular noun ends in any of these letters, its plural form remains unchanged:

- The plural of *le corps* (body) is *les corps* (bodies)
- The plural of *le prix* (price) is *les prix* (prices)
- The plural of *le nez* (nose) is *les nez* (noses)

Common words that end in *s* and *x* are:

- *l'ananas m.* (pineapple)
- *le bus* (bus)
- *le bas* (stocking)
- *le bras* (arm)
- *le colis* (package)
- *la fois* (time)
- *le héros* (hero)
- *le palais* (palace)

- *le pardessus* (overcoat)
- *le pays* (country)
- *le repas* (meal)
- *le tapis* (rug)
- *la voix* (voice)
- *la croix* (cross)

Other plurals are formed as follows:

- **Nouns ending in *eau* add *x* to form the plural:**

  le bateau (boat) becomes *les bateaux* (boats)

  le bureau (office, desk) becomes *les bureaux* (offices, desks)

  le cadeau (gift) becomes *les cadeaux* (gifts)

  le chapeau (hat) becomes *les chapeaux* (hats)

  le château (castle) becomes *les châteaux* (castles)

  le couteau (knife) becomes *les couteaux* (knives)

  le gâteau (cake) becomes *les gâteaux* (cakes)

  le manteau (coat) becomes *les manteaux* (coats)

  le morceau (piece) becomes *les morceaux* (pieces)

  l'oiseau m. (bird) becomes *les oiseaux* (birds)

  le rideau (curtain) becomes *les rideaux* (curtains)

- **Nouns ending in *eu* add *x* to form the plural, except that *le pneu* (tire) becomes *les pneus* (tires):**

  le cheveu (a single hair) becomes *les cheveux* (many hairs)

  le jeu (game) becomes *les jeux* (games)

  le lieu (place) becomes *les lieux* (places)

  le neveu (nephew) becomes *les neveux* (nephews)

■ **Nouns ending in *al* change *al* to *aux,* except for *le bal* (ball), which become *les bals* (balls), and *le festival* (the festival), which becomes *les festivals* (the festivals):**

> *l'animal* (animal) becomes *les animaux* (animals)
>
> *le cheval* (horse) becomes *les chevaux* (horses)
>
> *l'hôpital m.* (hospital) becomes *les hôpitaux* (hospitals)
>
> *le journal* (newspaper) becomes *les journaux* (newspapers)

■ **Some nouns ending in *ou* add *x* to form the plural:**

> *le bijou* (jewel) becomes *les bijoux* (jewels)
>
> *le genou* (knee) becomes *les genoux* (knees)
>
> *le joujou* (toy) becomes *les joujoux* (toys)

Useful irregular plurals include the following:

■ *l'œil m.* (eye) becomes *les yeux* (eyes)

■ *le travail* (work) becomes *les travaux* (works)

■ *madame* (Mrs.) becomes *mesdames*

■ *mademoiselle* (Miss) becomes *mesdemoiselles*

■ *monsieur* (Mr.) becomes *messieurs*

Most **compound nouns** (nouns made up of two nouns that are usually joined by a hyphen) do not change in the plural. Remember, however, to change their respective articles:

■ *l'après-midi m.* (afternoon) becomes *les après-midi* (afternoons)

■ *le gratte-ciel* (skyscraper) becomes *les gratte-ciel* (skyscrapers)

■ *le hors-d'œuvre* (appetizer) becomes *les hors-d'œuvre* (appetizers)

■ *le rendez-vous* (meeting) becomes *les rendez-vous* (meetings)

But:

■ *le grand-père* (grandfather) becomes *les grands-pères* (grandfathers)

■ *la grand-mère* (grandmother) becomes *les grands-mères* (grandmothers)

■ *le grand-parent* (grandparent) becomes *les grands-parents* (grandparents)

Just as in English, some words in French are always plural:

- *les ciseaux m.* (scissors)
- *les gens m.* (people)
- *les lunettes f.* (eyeglasses)
- *les mathématiques f.* (mathematics)
- *les vacances f.* (vacation)

Some nouns are singular but refer to a group of people. Make sure to use a singular verb that agrees with these subjects:

- *le public* (audience)
- *la foule* (crowd)
- *tout le monde* (everybody)
- *la famille* (family)
- *le groupe* (group)
- *la police* (police)

In French, last names do not add an *s* in the plural as they do in English:

- *Les Renard* (the Renards)
- *Les Lescaut* (the Lescauts)

Chapter Checkout

Change to the singular:

1. *les journaux*
2. *les grands-pères*
3. *les yeux*

Answers: 1. *le journal* **2.** *le grand-père* **3.** *l'œil*

Change to the plural:

4. *un gâteau*
5. *l'hôpital*

Answers: 4. *des gâteaux* **5.** *les hôpitaux*

Chapter 5
POSSESSION

Chapter Check-In

❑ Expressing possession with *de*

❑ Expressing possession using *être à*

❑ Using possessive adjectives

Possession shows that something or someone belongs to another person. In English, possession is often shown in writing by an apostrophe + s or by s + an apostrophe. This option does not exist in French because apostrophes are not used in the language to show possession.

In French, you can show possession or relationship in two ways: by using *de* to express "of" or by using possessive adjectives to express "my," "your," and so on.

Possession Using *de*

The preposition *de* (of) is used to express relationship and possession. If the sentence has two or more nouns, *de* (or *d'* before a vowel) is repeated before each noun: *Ce sont les parents de Roger et de Luc.* (They are Roger and Luke's parents./They are the parents of Roger and of Luke.)

With masculine singular and plural nouns, *de* contracts with the definite article *le* to become *du* or contracts with *les* to become *des* in order to express "of the":

■ *Ce sont les parents du garçon.* (They are the boy's parents./They are the parents of the boy.)

■ *Ce sont les parents des garçons.* (They are the boys' parents./They are the parents of the boys.)

Possession Using *être à*

The idiom *être à* (to belong to) is usually used to show possession of a thing. Conjugate *être* to agree with the subject, and if the sentence contains two or more nouns, repeat the preposition *à* before each noun: *Ces CDs sont à Mathieu et à Bernard.* (These CDs belong to Mathew and Bernard.)

Note how *être à* is used in questions, as follows:

- *À qui est ce stylo?* (Whose pen is this?)

- *À qui sont ces magazines?* (Whose magazines are these?)

Possessive Adjectives

Like all French adjectives, possessive adjectives, listed in Table 5-1, agree in gender and number with the nouns they modify (the person or item that is possessed) and not with the subject (the person possessing them).

Table 5-1   Possessive Adjectives

Singular Masculine	Singular Feminine	Plural	English
mon	ma	mes	my
ton	ta	tes	your
son	sa	ses	his, her, its
notre	notre	nos	our
votre	votre	vos	your
leur	leur	leurs	their

When using possessive adjectives, note the following:

- **Possessive adjectives agree with and are repeated before each noun.**

  J'aime mon père, ma mère, et mes sœurs. (I love my father, my mother, and my sisters.)

  Donne-moi leurs CDs et ta stéréo. (Give me their CDs and your stereo.)

■ *Son* and *sa* can mean either *his* or *her* because the possessive adjective agrees with the noun it modifies and not with the possessor. *Sa mère*, therefore, could mean either *his* or *her* mother, because *sa* agrees with the word *mother*, which is feminine. Similarly, *son père* can mean either *his* or *her* father because *son* agrees with the word *père*, which is masculine. The true meaning of the word can be determined only by the context of the conversation.

■ The forms *mon, ton,* and *son* are used instead of *ma, ta,* and *sa* before a feminine singular noun beginning with a vowel or vowel sound. This allows the words to flow smoothly.

> *mon adresse* (my address)
>
> *ton hôtesse* (your hostess)
>
> *son amie* (his/her friend)

■ When referring to parts of the body, the possessive adjective is generally replaced with the definite article if the possessor is clear.

> *Je me brosse les cheveux.* (I brush my hair.)
>
> *Elle lève la main.* (She raises her hand.)

■ There is no elision with possessive adjectives: The final *-a* from *ma, ta,* and *sa* may never be dropped.

> *Qui est ton artiste favorite?* (Who is your favorite artist?)

Some French expressions of relationship include the following:

■ *une de mes amies* (a [girl]friend of mine/one of my [girl]friends)

■ *un de ses enfants* (a child of his/one of his children)

■ *un de leurs voisins* (a neighbor of theirs/one of their neighbors)

Chapter Checkout

Answer each question using a possessive adjective and the noun:

1. Anne: *Jacqueline a de nouvelles robes. Elle va les prêter à sa sœur.*
   Paul: *Qu'est-ce qu'elle va prêter à sa sœur?*
   Anne: _____ _____

2. Anne: *J'ai un nouveau livre. Je vais le lire maintenant.*

Paul: *Qu'est-ce que tu vas lire maintenant?*

Anne: _____ _____

3. Anne: *Nous avons des devoirs à écrire. Nous pouvons les écrire ensemble.*

Paul: *Qu'est-ce que nous pouvons écrire ensemble?*

Anne: _____ _____

4. Anne: *Louis et Marie ont des parents vraiment gentils. Ils doivent les écouter.*

Paul: *Qui est-ce qu'ils doivent écouter?*

Anne: _____ _____

5. Anne: *Daniel a reçu une montre mais il l'a déjà perdue.*

Paul: *Qu'est-ce qu'il a perdu?*

Anne: _____ _____

Answers: 1. *ses robes* **2.** *mon livre* **3.** *nos devoirs* **4.** *leurs parents* **5.** *sa montre*

Chapter 6
PRONOUNS

Chapter Check-In

❏ Selecting subject pronouns

❏ Using object pronouns

❏ Using independent (stress) pronouns

❏ Using relative pronouns

A **pronoun** is a word that is used to replace a noun (a person, place, thing, idea, or quality). Pronouns allow for fluidity by eliminating the need to constantly repeat the same noun in a sentence.

Subject Pronouns

A **subject pronoun** replaces a **subject noun** (the noun performing the action of the verb). Just as in English, French subject pronouns are given a person and a number (singular or plural), as shown in Table 6-1:

Table 6-1   Subject Pronouns

Person	Singular	Plural
1st	*je* (I)	*nous* (we)
2nd	*tu* (you)	*vous* (you)
3rd	*il* (he, it)	*ils* (they)
	elle (she, it)	*elles* (they)
	on (one, you, we, they)	

Je

Unlike the English pronoun "I," the pronoun *je* is capitalized only when it begins a sentence. *Je* becomes *j'* before a vowel or vowel sound (*y* and **unaspirated** *h* — meaning that no puff of air is emitted when producing the "h" sound):

■ *J'adore le français.* (I love French.)

■ *Voilà où j'habite.* (There's where I live.)

Tu

Tu is used to address one friend, relative, child, or pet and is referred to as the familiar form of "you." The *u* from *tu* is never dropped for purposes of elision: *Tu es mon meilleur ami.* (You are my best friend.)

Vous

Vous is used in the singular to show respect to an older person or when speaking to a stranger or someone you do not know very well. *Vous* is the polite or formal form of "you": *Vous êtes un patron très respecté.* (You are a very respected boss.)

In addition, *vous* is always used when speaking to more than one person, regardless of the degree of familiarity.

Il and elle

Il (he) and *elle* (she) may refer to a person or to a thing (it):

■ *L'homme arrive.* (The man arrives.) *Il arrive.* (He arrives.)

■ *Le colis arrive.* (The package arrives.) *Il arrive.* (It arrives.)

■ *La dame arrive.* (The lady arrives.) *Elle arrive.* (She arrives.)

■ *La lettre arrive.* (The letter arrives.) *Elle arrive.* (It arrives.)

On

On refers to an indefinite person: you, we, they, or people in general. *On* is often used in place of *nous,* such as in the following: *On part.* (We're leaving.)

Ils and *elles*

Ils refers to more than one male or to a combined group of males and females, despite the number of each gender present. *Elles* refers only to a group of females.

- *Anne et Luc partent.* (Ann and Luke leave.) *Ils partent.* (They leave.)

- *Anne et Marie partent.* (Ann and Marie leave.) *Elles partent.* (They leave.)

Ce

The pronoun *ce* (it, he, she, this, that, these, those), spelled *c'* before a vowel, is most frequently used with the verb *être* (to be): *c'est* (it is) or *ce sont* (they are). *Ce* replaces *il, elle, ils,* and *elles* as the subject of the sentence in the following constructions:

- **Before a modified noun:** *C'est un bon avocat.* (He's a good lawyer.)

  But, when unmodified, the following is correct: *Il est avocat.* (He's a lawyer.)

- **Before a name:** *C'est Jean.* (It's John.)

- **Before a pronoun:** *C'est moi.* (It is me.)

- **Before a superlative:** *C'est le plus grand.* (It's the biggest.)

- **In dates:** *C'est le dix mars.* (It's March 10th.)

- **To refer to a previously mentioned idea or action:** *Il est important.* (He is important.) *C'est évident.* (That's obvious).

- **Before an adjective + *à* + infinitive (the form of any verb before it is conjugated — see Chapter 7):** *C'est bon à savoir.* (That's good to know.)

Use *il* in the following constructions:

- **To express the hour of the day:** *Il est deux heures.* (It's 2:00.)

- **With an adjective + *de* + infinitive:** *Il est bon de manger.* (It's good to eat.)

- **With an adjective before *que*:** *Il est important que je travaille.* (It is important that I work.)

Object Pronouns

Object pronouns are used so that an object noun doesn't have to be continuously repeated. This allows for a more free-flowing conversational tone. When using object pronouns, make sure your conjugated verb (see Chapter 7) agrees with the subject and not the object pronoun. Table 6-2 lists direct and indirect object pronouns:

Table 6-2   Direct/Indirect Object Pronouns

Direct	Indirect
me [m'] (me)	me [m'] (to me)
te [t'] (you)	te [t'] (to you)
le [l'] (he, it)	lui (to him)
la [l'] (her, it)	lui (to her)
nous (us)	nous (to us)
vous (you)	vous (to you)
les (them)	leur (to them)
se [s'] (themselves)	se [s'] (to themselves)

The forms *me, te, se, nous,* and *vous* are both direct and indirect objects and reflexive pronouns (see Chapter 17).

Direct object pronouns

Direct objects (which can be nouns or pronouns) answer the question to whom or what the subject is acting upon. It may refer to people, places, things, or ideas. A direct object pronoun replaces a direct object noun and, unlike in English, is usually placed before the conjugated verb.

- *Tu regardes le film.* (You watch the movie.) *Tu le regardes.* (You watch it.)
- *Je t'aime.* (I love you.)
- *Tu m'aimes.* (You love me.)

Indirect object pronouns

Indirect objects (which can be nouns or pronouns) answer the question to or for whom the subject is doing something. They refer only to people. An indirect object pronoun replaces an indirect object noun, and, unlike in English, is usually placed before the conjugated verb. As a clue, look for the preposition *à* (to, for), which may be in the form of *au* (the contraction of *à* + *le*), *à l'*, *à la*, or *aux* (the contraction of *à* + *les*), followed by the name or reference to a person.

- *Elle écrit à Jean.* (She writes to John.) *Elle lui écrit.* (She writes to him.)
- *Tu m'offres un sac à main.* (You offer me a purse.)
- *Je t'offre un sac à main.* (I offer you a purse.)

Verbs that take an indirect object in English do not necessarily take an indirect object in French. The following verbs take a direct object in French:

- *attendre* (to wait for)
- *chercher* (to look for)
- *écouter* (to listen to)
- *espérer* (to hope for/to)
- *faire venir* (to call for)
- *payer* (to pay)

Verbs that take a direct object in English do not necessarily take a direct object in French. The following verbs take an indirect object in French because they are followed by *à*:

- *convenir à* (to suit)
- *désobéir à* (to disobey)
- *faire honte à* (to shame)
- *faire mal à* (to hurt)
- *faire peur à* (to frighten)
- *obéir à* (to obey)
- *plaire à* (to please)
- *répondre à* (to answer)
- *ressembler à* (to resemble)
- *téléphoner à* (to call)

The expression *penser à* (to think about) is followed by a stress pronoun, described in the "Independent (Stress) Pronouns" section of this chapter; for example, *Je pense à lui/elle.* (I think about him/her.)

The following verbs require an indirect object because they are followed by *à*. Note the correct preposition to use before the infinitive of the verb.

- *apprendre* (teach) *à quelqu'un à* + infinitive

- *enseigner* (teach) *à quelqu'un à* + infinitive

- *conseiller* (advise) *à quelqu'un de* + infinitive

- *défendre* (forbid) *à quelqu'un de* + infinitive

- *demander* (ask) *à quelqu'un de* + infinitive

- *ordonner* (order) *à quelqu'un de* + infinitive

- *pardonner* (forgive) *à quelqu'un de* + infinitive

- *permettre* (permit) *à quelqu'un de* + infinitive

- *promettre* (promise) *à quelqu'un de* + infinitive

- *rappeler* (remind) *à quelqu'un de* + infinitive

- *reprocher* (reproach) *à quelqu'un de* + infinitive

With the French verbs *plaire* (to please), *falloir* (to be necessary), and *manquer* (to miss), the French indirect object is the subject in the English sentence:

- *Ce cadeau me plaît.* (I like this gift. This gift is pleasing to me.)

- *Il me faut un stylo.* (I need a pen. A pen is necessary for me.)

- *Tu me manques.* (I miss you. You are missing to me.)

The adverbial pronoun (y)

The adverbial pronoun *y* (pronounced ee) means "there" when the place has already been mentioned. *Y* can also mean "it," "them," "in it/them," "to it/them," or "on it/them." *Y* usually replaces the preposition *à* + the noun object of the preposition, but it may also replace other prepositions of location or position, such as *chez* (at the house/business of), *dans* (in), *en* (in), *sous* (under), or *sur* (on) + noun:

- *Je vais à Paris.* (I'm going to Paris.) *J'y vais.* (I'm going there.)

- *Il répond à la note.* (He answers the note.) *Il y répond.* (He answers it.)

- *Tu restes dans ton lit.* (You stay in your bed.) *Tu y restes.* (You stay in it.)

Y is used to replace *de* + noun only when *de* is part of a prepositional phrase showing location: *L'hôtel est près de l'aéroport.* (The hotel is near the airport.) *L'hôtel y est.* (The hotel is there.)

Never use *y* to replace *à* + a person. Indirect object pronouns are used for this purpose: *Je parle à Luc.* (I speak to Luke.) *Je lui parle.* (I speak to him.)

Sometimes *y* is used in French but is not translated into English: *Il va au cinéma?* (Is he going to the movies?) *Oui, il y va.* (Yes, he is.)

The adverbial pronoun *(en)*

The pronoun *en* refers to previously mentioned things or places. *En* usually replaces *de* + noun and may mean "some" or "any," "of it/them," "about it/them," "from it/them," or "from there":

- *Je veux de la glace.* (I want some ice cream.) *J'en veux.* (I want some [of it].)

- *Tu ne bois pas de lait.* (You don't drink any milk.) *Tu n'en bois pas.* (You don't drink any.)

- *Il parle de l'examen.* (He speaks about the test.) *Il en parle.* (He speaks about it.)

- *Vous sortez du café.* (You leave the cafe.) *Vous en sortez.* (You leave [from] it.)

En is always expressed in French even though it may have no English equivalent or is not expressed in English: *As-tu du temps?* (Do you have any time?) *Oui, j'en ai.* (Yes, I do.)

Note the following rules governing the use of *en:*

- ***En* is used with idiomatic expressions requiring *de*.**

  J'ai besoin de film. (I need film.) *J'en ai besoin.* (I need some.)

- ***En* is used to replace a noun after a number or a noun or adverb of quantity (*de* + noun).**

  Je prépare six gâteaux. (I'm preparing six cakes.) *J'en prépare six.* (I'm preparing six [of them].)

  Tu bois une tasse de thé. (You drink a cup of tea.) *Tu en bois.* (You drink a cup [of it].)

■ *En* only refers to people when *de* means "some." In all other cases (when *de* + a noun means "of" or "about" a person), a stress pronoun is used.

> *J'ai beaucoup de fils.* (I have a lot of sons.) *J'en ai beaucoup.* (I have a lot of them.)

The position of object pronouns

An object pronoun is placed before the verb to which its meaning is tied, usually before the conjugated verb (see Chapter 7). When a sentence contains two verbs, the object pronoun is placed before the infinitive:

■ *Je le demande.* (I ask for it.) *Je ne le demande pas.* (I don't ask for it.)

■ *Il va en boire.* (He is going to drink some of it.) *Il ne va pas en boire.* (He isn't going to drink some of it.)

In an affirmative command, an object pronoun is placed immediately after the verb and is joined to it by a hyphen. The familiar command forms of *-er* verbs (regular and irregular — see Chapter 7) retain their final *s* before *y* and *en* to prevent the clash of two vowel sounds together. Put a liaison (linking) between the final consonant and *y* or *en*: *Restes-y!* (Stay there!) But: *N'y reste pas!* (Don't stay there!)

In compound tenses, the object pronoun is placed before the conjugated helping verb (see Chapter 7): *J'ai parlé à Nancy.* (I spoke to Nancy.) *Je lui ai parlé.* (I spoke to her.)

Double object pronouns

The term **double object pronouns** refers to using more than one pronoun in a sentence at a time, as follows:

Order Before the Verb

me				
te				
se	*le (l')*	*lui*	*y*	*en* + verb
nous	*la (l')*	*leur*		
vous	*les*			
se				

Order After the Verb (Affirmative Commands)

	-moi			
	-toi			
	-le	-lui	-y	-en
verb +	-la	-nous		
	-les	-vous		
	-leur			

The following examples show how double object pronouns are used before the conjugated verb, before the infinitive when there are two verbs, in the past tense, and in a negative command. Note the different order of the pronouns in the affirmative command:

- **Before the conjugated verb:** *Elle me la donne.* (She gives it to me.)

- **Before the infinitive with two verbs:** *Vas-tu m'en offrir?* (Are you going to offer me any?)

- **In the past tense:** *Tu le lui as écrit.* (You wrote it to her.)

- **In a negative command:** *Ne me le montrez pas.* (Don't show it to me.)

But note the difference in an affirmative command: *Montrez-le-moi, s'il vous plaît.* (Please show it to me.)

In an affirmative command, *moi + en* and *toi + en* become *m'en* and *t'en*, respectively:

- *Donne-m'en, s'il te plaît.* (Please give me some.)

- *Va t'en.* (Go away.)

Independent (Stress) Pronouns

Independent pronouns, listed in Table 6-3, may stand alone or follow a verb or a preposition. They are used to emphasize a fact and to highlight or replace nouns or pronouns.

Table 6-3   Independent Pronouns

Singular	Plural
moi (I, me)	*nous* (we, us)
toi (you)	*vous* (you)
lui (he, him)	*eux* (they, them)
elle (she, her)	*elles* (they, them)
soi (oneself)	

Independent pronouns are used as follows:

■ **To stress the subject:** *Moi, je suis vraiment indépendant.* (Me, I'm really independent.)

■ **When the pronoun has no verb:** *Qui veut partir?* (Who wants to leave?) *Moi.* (Me.)

■ **After prepositions to refer to a person or persons:** *Allons chez elle.* (Let's go to her house.)

■ **After** *c'est:* *C'est moi qui pars.* (I'm leaving.)

■ **After the following verbs:**

   avoir affaire à (to have dealings with)

   être à (to belong to)

   faire attention à (to pay attention to)

   penser à (to think about [of])

   se fier à (to trust)

   s'intéresser à (to be interested in)

■ **In compound subjects:**

   Lui et moi allons au restaurant. (He and I are going to the restaurant.)

   Sylvie et toi dînez chez Marie. (Sylvia and you are dining at Marie's.)

If *moi* is one of the stress pronouns in a compound subject, the subject pronoun *nous* is used in summary (someone + me = we) and the conjugated verb must agree with *nous*. If *toi* is one of the stress pronouns in a compound subject, the subject prounoun *vous* is used in summary (someone + you [singular] = you [plural]) and the conjugated verb must agree with the *vous*. Neither *nous* nor *vous* has to appear in the sentence.

■ **With -*même(s)* to reinforce the subject:** *Je suis allé au concert moi-même.* (I went to the concert by myself.)

Relative Pronouns

A **relative pronoun** ("who," "which," or "that") joins a main clause to a dependent clause. This pronoun introduces the dependent clause that describes someone or something mentioned in the main clause. The person or thing the pronoun refers to is called the **antecedent.** A relative clause may serve as a subject, a direct object, or an object of a preposition.

Qui (subject) and *que* (direct object)

Qui ("who," "which," "that") is the subject of a relative clause (which means that it will be followed by a verb in the dependent clause). *Qui* may refer to people, things, or places and follows the format **antecedent + subject + <u>verb</u>**: *C'est **la femme** qui <u>a gagné</u>.* (She's the woman who won.)

The verb of a relative clause introduced by *qui* is conjugated to agree with its antecedent: *C'est moi qui choisis les bons cafés.* (I am the one who chooses the good cafés.)

Que ("whom," "which," or "that") is the direct object of a relative clause (which means that it will be followed by a noun or pronoun). Although frequently omitted in English, the relative pronoun is always expressed in French. *Que* may refer to people or things and follows the format **antecedent + direct object + <u>pronoun</u>**: *C'est **l'homme** que <u>j'adore</u>.* (He's the man [that] I love.)

Qui and *lequel* (objects of a preposition)

Qui (meaning "whom") is used as the object of a preposition referring to a person.

> *Anne est la femme avec qui je travaille.* (Anne is the woman with whom I am working.)

Lequel, laquelle, lesquels, and *lesquelles* ("which" or "whom") are used as the object of a preposition referring primarily to things. The form of *lequel* must agree with the antecedent. Select the proper form of *lequel* after consulting Table 6-4, for example, *Voilà la piscine dans laquelle je nage.* (There is the pool in which I swim.)

Table 6-4   Forms of *Lequel*

	Singular	Plural
Masculine	lequel	lesquels
Feminine	laquelle	lesquelles

Lequel and its forms contract with the prepositions *à* and *de,* as shown in Table 6-5:

Table 6-5   *Lequel* with Prepositions

Singular		Plural	
Masculine	**Feminine**	**Masculine**	**Feminine**
auquel	à laquelle	auxquels	auxquelles
duquel	de laquelle	desquels	desquelles

Some examples include the following:

■ *Ce sont les hommes auxquels elle pense.* (Those are the men she is thinking about.)

■ *C'est la classe de laquelle je parlais.* (That's the class I was talking about.)

Ce qui and *ce que*

The relative pronouns *ce qui* and *ce que* are used when no antecedent noun or pronoun is present:

■ ***Ce qui* means "what" or "that which" and is the subject of a verb:** *Je me demande ce qui se passe.* (I wonder what is happening.)

■ ***Ce que* means "what" (that which) and is the object of a verb:** *Tu sais ce que ça veut dire.* (You know what that means.)

Chapter Checkout

Rewrite the sentence replacing the underlined word(s) with the correct pronoun:

1. *Elles vont <u>chez Marie et Luc.</u>*

2. *Prends <u>du café.</u>*

3. *Nous <u>restons á Nice.</u>*

Answers: 1. *Elles y vont.* **2.** *Prends-en.* **3.** *Nous y restons.*

Fill in the missing word:

4. *C'est un homme _____ est intéressant.*

5. *Montrez-moi _____ est dans le bureau.*

Answers: 4. *qui* **5.** *ce qui*

Chapter 7

THE PRESENT TENSE OF VERBS

Chapter Check-In

❑ Forming the present tense

❑ Using idiomatic expressions

❑ Commanding others

To form the present tense (that is, what is happening, what does happen, or what happens now) in French, verbs must be **conjugated:** the ending of the verb must be changed so that it agrees with the subject (noun or pronoun) performing the task. Although this is done automatically by native speakers in their language, conjugating French verbs for the first time takes some thought and practice. Some verbs follow a pattern and are called **regular;** others do not follow any pattern and are considered **irregular.** A few verb endings require spelling changes within the verb.

In addition, some verbs are used in **idiomatic expressions,** which defy a word-by-word translation or a grammatical explanation but do lend color to the language.

Finally, present tense verb forms are used to issue commands, such as those you need when giving directions.

The Infinitive Form

A verb expresses an action or state of being and is generally shown in its **infinitive,** which is the basic "to" form, as in "to be." An infinitive is the form of the verb before it has been conjugated.

Table 7-1 shows an example of the irregular verb "to be" conjugated in English.

Table 7-1   Conjugation of "to Be" in English

	Singular	*Plural*
1st person	I am	We are
2nd person	You are	You are
3rd person	He is	They are
	She is	They are

Even in English, each subject has its own matching verb form that never changes and can't be mixed and matched with other verb forms.

Regular Verbs

In French, regular verbs are grouped into three main families (*-er, -ir,* and *-re*) because these are their endings in the infinitive form. Each regular verb within its respective family then follows the same rules of conjugation. If you memorize the pattern for one family, you know the pattern for all the verbs within that family. To form the present tense of *-er, -ir,* and *-re* verbs, drop the infinitive ending (the final *-er,* the final *-ir,* or the final *-re*) and add the endings for the subject pronouns indicated, as shown in Tables 7-2, 7-3, and 7-4.

Table 7-2   *-er* Verb Rules of Conjugation Using *Parler* (to Speak)

je	*tu*	*il, elle*	*nous*	*vous*	*ils, elles*
-e	-es	-e	-ons	-ez	-ent
parle	parles	parle	parlons	parlez	parlent

Table 7-3   *-ir* Verb Rules of Conjugation Using *Finir* (to Finish)

je	*tu*	*il, elle*	*nous*	*vous*	*ils, elles*
-is	-is	-it	-issons	-issez	-issent
finis	finis	finit	finissons	finissez	finissent

Table 7-4 *-re* **Verb Rules of Conjugation Using** *Vendre* **(to Sell)**

je	tu	il, elle	nous	vous	ils, elles
-s	-s	-	-ons	-ez	-ent
vends	vends	vend	vendons	vendez	vendent

Three exceptions to the *-re* verb rule include *rompre* (to break), *corrompre* (to corrupt), and *interrompre* (to interrupt). They end in *-t* in the third person singular: *il rompt, il corrompt,* and *il interrompt.*

The present tense verb form expresses action: "I play," "I do play" (do + verb), or "I am playing" (to be + verb). The verbs "to do" and "to be" are used only when they stand alone, as seen later in this chapter in the section called "Irregular Verbs."

Regular Verbs with Spelling Changes

Verbs with certain spelling changes and irregularities are referred to as **shoe verbs** (spelling-change verbs) because changes and irregularities occur for pronouns located either within or outside the imaginary shoe. The *nous* and *vous* forms of the verb are usually, but not always, those that resemble the infinitive.

Figure 7-1 The shoe verbs.

Shoes Verbs

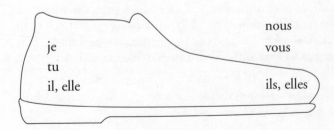

The following groups of verbs are considered shoe verbs. Observe the special changes that each requires. Note that sometimes changes occur outside the shoe in the *nous* or the *nous* and *vous* forms; at other times, the changes occur within the shoe.

■ **For verbs ending in *-cer*, change *c* to *ç* before *a* or *o* to keep the soft *c* (s) sound:**

> *avancer* (to advance): *j'avance, tu avances, il avance, nous avançons, vous avancez, ils avancent*

> Other *-cer* verbs include *annoncer* (to announce), *commencer* (to begin), *menacer* (to threaten), *placer, remplacer* (to replace), and *renoncer à* (to renounce).

■ **For verbs ending in *-ger*, insert a silent *e* between *g* and *a* and between *g* and *o* to keep the soft *g* (zh) sound:**

> *manger* (to eat): *je mange, tu manges, il mange, nous mangeons, vous mangez, ils mangent*

> Other *-ger* verbs include *arranger* (to arrange), *changer* (to change), *corriger* (to correct), *déranger* (to disturb), *diriger* (to direct), *nager* (to swim), *obliger* (to force), *partager* (to share), and *ranger* (to tidy).

■ **In *-yer* verbs, the *y* is kept in the *nous* and *vous* forms except for *-ayer* verbs, where the change is optional.** An *i* is used instead of *y* within the shoe. Verbs ending in *-ayer* include *payer* and *essayer [de]* (to try [to]).

> *employer* (to use, employ): *j'emploie, tu emploies, il emploie, nous employons, vous employez, ils emploient*

> Other *-yer* verbs include *ennuyer* (to bother), *envoyer* (to send), and *nettoyer* (to clean).

■ **For silent *e* + consonant + *-er* verbs, change the silent *e* to *è* for all forms in the shoe.** The addition of an accent grave (*è*) to the silent *e* gives it an *eh* sound and the verb ending remains silent. This avoids having two consecutive silent vowels, which would make the verb virtually impossible to pronounce.

> *acheter* (to buy): *j'achète, tu achètes, il achète, nous achetons, vous achetez, ils achètent*

> Other verbs in this category include *achever* (to finish), *amener* (to bring, lead to), *emmener* (to take, lead away), *enlever* (to take off, remove), *peser* (to weigh), and *promener* (to walk).

■ For *appeler* (to call) and *jeter* (to throw), double the consonant that comes before the *-er* ending instead of adding an accent grave:

> *j'appelle, tu appelles, il appelle, nous appelons, vous appelez, ils appellent*
>
> *je jette, tu jettes, il jette, nous jetons, vous jetez, ils jettent*

■ For *é* + consonant + *-er* verbs, change *é* to *è* within the shoe only:

> *répéter* (to repeat): *je répète, tu répètes, il répète, nous répétons, vous répétez, ils répètent*

> Other verbs in this form include *célébrer* (to celebrate), *espérer* (to hope), *posséder* (to possess), *préférer* (to prefer), and *protéger* (to protect).

Irregular Verbs

Many high-frequency French verbs are irregular, which means that they follow no specific rules of conjugation and must be memorized. The most common irregular verbs are as follows:

■ *aller* (to go): *je vais, tu vas, il va, nous allons, vous allez, ils vont*

■ *avoir* (to have): *j'ai, tu as, il a, nous avons, vous avez, ils ont*

■ *boire* (to drink): *je bois, tu bois, il boit, nous buvons, vous buvez, ils boivent*

■ *conduire* (to drive): *je conduis, tu conduis, il conduit, nous conduisons, vous conduisez, ils conduisent*

■ *connaître* (to know, be acquainted with): *je connais, tu connais, il connaît, nous connaissons, vous connaissez, ils connaissent*

■ *croire* (to believe): *je crois, tu crois, il croit, nous croyons, vous croyez, ils croient*

■ *devoir* (to have to, to owe): *je dois, tu dois, il doit, nous devons, vous devez, ils doivent*

■ *dire* (to say, tell): *je dis, tu dis, il dit, nous disons, vous dites, ils disent*

■ *dormir* (**to sleep**): *je dors, tu dors, il dort, nous dormons, vous dormez, ils dorment.* Verbs like *dormir* keep the consonant before the -*ir* ending in all plural forms: *mentir* (to lie), *partir* (to go away), *sentir* (to feel, smell), *servir* (to serve), *sortir* (to go out).

■ *écrire* (**to write**): *j'écris, tu écris, il écrit, nous écrivons, vous écrivez, ils écrivent*

■ *être* (**to be**): *je suis, tu es, il est, nous sommes, vous êtes, ils sont*

■ *faire* (**to make, do**): *je fais, tu fais, il fait, nous faisons, vous faites, ils font*

■ *lire* (**to read**): *je lis, tu lis, il lit, nous lisons, vous lisez, ils lisent*

■ *mettre* (**to put [on]**): *je mets, tu mets, il met, nous mettons, vous mettez, ils mettent.* Verbs like *mettre* include *commettre* (to commit), *permettre* (to permit), *promettre* (to promise), and *remettre* (to put back).

■ *offrir* (**to offer**): *j'offre, tu offres, il offre, nous offrons, vous offrez, ils offrent*

■ *ouvrir* (**to open**): *j'ouvre, tu ouvres, il ouvre, nous ouvrons, vous ouvrez, ils ouvrent*

■ *pouvoir* (**to be able to**): *je peux, tu peux, il peut, nous pouvons, vous pouvez, ils peuvent*

■ *prendre* (**to take**): *je prends, tu prends, il prend, nous prenons, vous prenez, ils prennent.* Verbs like *prendre* include *apprendre* (to learn) and *comprendre* (to understand).

■ *recevoir* (**to receive**): *je reçois, tu reçois, il reçoit, nous recevons, vous recevez, ils reçoivent*

■ *savoir* (**to know a fact**): *je sais, tu sais, il sait, nous savons, vous savez, ils savent*

■ *venir* (**to come**): *je viens, tu viens, il vient, nous venons, vous venez, ils viennent.* Verbs like *venir* include *devenir* (to become) and *revenir* (to come back).

■ *voir* (**to see**): *je vois, tu vois, il voit, nous voyons, vous voyez, ils voient*

■ *vouloir* (**to wish, want**): *je veux, tu veux, il veut, nous voulons, vous voulez, ils veulent*

Idiomatic Expressions

An **idiom** is a particular word or expression whose meaning cannot be readily understood by either its grammar or the words used. Idiomatic expressions cannot be translated word for word without causing confusion. For example, when combined with an adverb that describes feeling or health, *aller* (to go) is used to describe a person's health: *Je vais bien.* (I feel fine. I'm fine.)

Although the verb "to be" is used in English to refer to certain physical conditions, in French you express the same thought by combining the verb *avoir* (to have) with a noun:

- *avoir . . . ans* (to be . . . years old)
- *avoir l'air* (to appear)
- *avoir besoin de* (to need)
- *avoir chaud* (to be hot)
- *avoir de la chance* (to be lucky)
- *avoir froid* (to be cold)
- *avoir envie de* (to feel like, to want)
- *avoir faim* (to be hungry)
- *avoir soif* (to be thirsty)
- *avoir lieu* (to take place)
- *avoir mal à* (to have an ache)
- *avoir peur [de]* (to be afraid of)
- *avoir raison* (to be right)
- *avoir tort* (to be wrong)
- *avoir sommeil* (to be sleepy)

Three important idioms using *être* (to be) are as follows:

- *être à* (to belong to)
- *être en train de* (to be in the act [middle] of)
- *être sur le point de* (to be on the verge of)

Some idioms with *faire* (to do or make) include the following:

- *faire attention (à)* (to pay attention to)

- *faire la connaissance de* (to meet or make the acquaintance of someone)

- *faire un voyage* (to take a trip)

Faire is also used idiomatically to describe the weather and sports, as follows:

- *Quel temps fait-il?* (What's the weather?)

- *Il fait beau.* (It's beautiful.)

- *Luc fait du ski.* (Luke goes skiing.)

Combining *venir de* (to [have] just) with an infinitive shows that the subject has just done something: *Je viens de manger.* (I just ate.) Keep in mind that when two verbs are used in succession, the first verb is conjugated and the second verb remains in the infinitive: *Je veux sortir.* (I want to go out.)

Finally, use the present tense idiomatically as follows:

- **Use it instead of the future to ask for instructions or to discuss an action that will happen in the near future.**

  Je sors? (Shall I go out?)

  Il part tout à l'heure. (He's leaving soon.)

- **To express an event that began in the past and is continuing in the present, use the following formula: present tense + *depuis* + expression of time.**

  Je souffre depuis hier. (I've been suffering since yesterday.)

- **The construction *il y a* + expression of time + *que* + present tense also expresses an action begun in the past and continuing in the present.**

  Il y a six ans qu'elle danse. (She's been dancing for six years.)

Commands

"You" is the understood subject of a command and is, therefore, omitted. (*Tu* and *vous* are the two ways to say "you" in French.) Use *tu*, the familiar command, when speaking to one friend or family member. Use *vous*, the polite command, when speaking formally or when directing the command to more than one person. To form a command, simply drop the subject pronoun and use the proper verb form that would match the pronoun you are dropping:

- *Regarde le panneau!* (Look at the sign!)
- *Descendez du train!* (Get off the train!)

Note that the *tu* command of *-er* verbs drops the final *s* from the conjugated verb in both regular and irregular verbs except when followed by the adverbial pronouns *y* (there) and *en* (some, of, about, from, it or them) See Chapter 6 for more about *y* and *en*.

- *Vas-y.* (Go there.)
- *Manges-en.* (Eat some of it.)

Three common irregular verb commands are shown in Table 7-5. The *nous* form of the verb (without the subject) may be used to suggest "let's": *Allons au cinema.* (Let's go to the movies.)

Table 7-5   Irregular Verb Commands

	avoir	*être*	*savoir*
tu	*aie*	*sois*	*sache*
nous	*ayons*	*soyons*	*sachons*
vous	*ayez*	*soyez*	*sachez*

Chapter Checkout

Give the correct form of the verb:

1. *Je m'(appeller)* _____ *Jean.*

2. *J'(avoir)* _____ *vingt ans.*

3. *Je (être)* _____ *intelligent.*

4. *Je (aller)* _____ *à la bibliothèque et je (faire)* _____ *des études.*

5. *Je (vouloir)* _____ *devenir docteur.*

Answers: 1. *appelle* 2. *ai* 3. *suis* 4. *vais, fais* 5. *veux*

Chapter 8

NEGATION

Chapter Check-In

❑ Using negatives

❑ Using negative expressions

Negatives express not, never, neither . . . nor, no longer, no more, no one, nobody, only, and nothing.

Like English, double negatives are not used in French; however, in French, a negative is generally made up of two parts, which must be placed properly. Forming the negative may or may not include the word *non* (no).

In addition, certain negative expressions are used colloquially and idiomatically and are necessary parts of everyday conversation.

Common Negative Words and Phrases

Of the most commonly used negatives, listed in Table 8-1, *ne . . . pas* is the most frequently used. Consider the following examples:

- *Je ne fume pas.* (I don't smoke.)
- *Elle ne conduit jamais.* (She never drives.)

Table 8-1   Common Negatives

Negative	English Translation
ne . . . jamais	never
ne . . . ni . . . ni	neither . . . nor
ne . . . pas	not

Negative	English Translation
ne . . . personne	no one, nobody, anyone, anybody
ne . . . plus	no more, no longer
ne . . . que	only
ne . . . rien	nothing

Some words used in questions produce a logical negative response, as in the following examples. Table 8-2 contains more logical negative responses.

- *Tu cherches quelqu'un?* (Are you looking for someone?)

- *Je ne cherche personne.* (I'm not looking for anyone.)

Table 8-2   Logical Negative Responses

Question Words	Negative Response
quelqu'un (someone, somebody)	*ne . . . personne* (no one, nobody, anyone, anybody)
quelquefois (sometimes)	*ne . . . jamais* (never)
quelque chose (something)	*ne . . . rien* (nothing)
toujours (always)	*ne . . . jamais* (never)
toujours (still)	*ne . . . plus* (no more, no longer)

Some high frequency negative expressions include the following:

- ***ça ne fait rien* (it doesn't matter)**

    Tu es en retard. (You're late.) *Ça ne fait rien.* (It doesn't matter.)

- ***de rien* (you're welcome) and *il n'y a pas de quoi* (you're welcome)**

    Merci beaucoup. (Thanks a lot.) *De rien. [Il n'y a pas de quoi.]* (You're welcome.)

- ***jamais de la vie!* (never! out of the question! not on your life!)**

    Tu veux piloter un avion? (Do you want to pilot an airplane?) *Jamais de la vie!* (Not on your life!)

- *pas du tout* (not at all)

    Ça vous énerve? (Does that bother you?) *Pas du tout.* (Not at all.)

- *pas encore* (not yet)

    Tu veux manger? (Do you want to eat?) *Pas encore.* (Not yet.)

- *pas maintenant* (not now)

    On sort? (Shall we go out?) *Pas maintenant.* (Not yet.)

Forming the Negative

In simple tenses (present, imperfect, future, conditional) and in the compound past tense *(le passé composé), ne* precedes the conjugated verb (the conjugated form of *avoir* or *être* in the *passé composé*), and any pronouns, including reflexive pronouns. The second part of the negative follows the conjugated verb (or follows the subject pronoun in an inverted question). Table 8-3 illustrates how this is done. If you need a review of conjugating verbs, check out Chapters 7, 14, 15, 16, and 17.

Table 8-3   Positioning the Negative

Tense	French Negation	English Translation
Present tense	*Je ne fume pas.* *Ne fumes-tu pas?*	I don't smoke. Don't you smoke?
Present tense with two verbs	*Je ne vais jamais fumer.*	I'm never going to smoke.
Command in the present tense	*Ne fume pas!*	Don't smoke!
Reflexive	*Il ne se rase jamais.*	He never shaves.
Imperfect	*Je ne fumais rien.*	I wasn't smoking anything.
Future	*Je ne fumerai plus.*	I will no longer smoke.
Conditional	*Je ne fumerais que des cigarettes.*	I would smoke only cigarettes.
Passé composé	*Je n'ai jamais fumé.*	I never smoked.
Reflexive *passé composé*	*Il ne s'est pas rasé.*	He didn't shave.

Consider the following rules regarding the formation of negatives:

■ *Ne* + the negative goes around the conjugated verb when it is followed by an infinitive.

> *Elle ne veut plus jouer.* (She doesn't want to play anymore.)
>
> *Il ne peut pas sortir.* (He can't go out.)

■ *Personne* follows the past participle and the infinitive:

> *Il n'a vu personne.* (He didn't see anyone.)
>
> *Je ne veux voir personne.* (I don't want to see anyone.)

■ *Que* precedes the word or words stressed.

> *Il ne mange que deux fois par jour.* (He eats only two times a day.)
>
> *Elle n'a acheté qu'une robe.* (She bought only one dress.)
>
> *Je ne vais le faire qu'une fois.* (I'm going to do it only once.)

■ Each part of the *ne . . . ni . . . ni* construction precedes the word or words stressed.

> *Nous ne mangeons ni viande ni poisson.* (We eat neither meat nor fish.)
>
> *Le cours n'était ni bon ni mauvais.* (The course was neither good nor bad.)
>
> *Il n'a ni étudié ni fait ses devoirs.* (He neither studied nor did his homework.)

■ *Rien* and *personne* may be used as subjects of a verb, with *ne* remaining before the conjugated verb.

> *Rien n'est arrivé.* (Nothing happened.)
>
> *Personne n'est arrivé.* (Nobody arrived.)

■ *Ne* is always used with a verb. The second part of the negative, however, may be used alone (without *ne*). *Pas* and *plus* must be modified.

> *Qu'est-ce que tu manges?* (What are you eating?) *Rien.* (Nothing.)
>
> *Qui chante?* (Who's singing?) *Personne.* (No one.)

Tu aimes le film? (Do you like the film?) *Pas beaucoup.* (Not much.)

Plus de gâteau pour toi. (No more cake for you.)

■ *Ne . . . jamais* used with a verb and *jamais* used alone without a verb mean "never." *Jamais* with only a verb means "ever."

Je n'ai jamais vu ce film. (I never saw that film.) *Non, jamais!* (No, never!)

Es-tu jamais allé au Canada? (Have you ever been to Canada?)

Chapter Checkout

Write the negative expression that you might use in response to the following:

1. *Merci beaucoup pour le cadeau.*
2. *On joue au basket?*
3. *Pardon. Je suis en retard.*
4. *Ça t'énerve si je mange du chocolat?*
5. *Tu veux nager dans l'océan pendant l'hiver?*

Answers: 1. *De rien./Il n'y a pas de quoi.* **2.** *Pas encore./Pas maintenant.* **3.** *Ça ne fait rien.* **4.** *Pas du tout.* **5.** *Jamais de la vie!*

Chapter 9

INTERROGATIVES AND EXCLAMATIONS

Chapter Check-In

❑ Asking yes or no questions

❑ Asking for information

❑ Using *il y a*

❑ Exclaiming

You can ask two types of questions: those that ask for a *yes* or *no* answer and those that ask for information. And you can ask each type of question in several ways: Some are more colloquial than others and are usually used when speaking; others are used more formally and when writing. Yes or no questions are formed by adding question marks, using the tag *n'est-ce pas,* using *est-ce que,* or using inversion. Questions that ask for information are formed by using interrogative adjectives, adverbs, and pronouns.

In addition, exclamations are used to show surprise, delight, incredulity, emphasis, or other strong emotion.

Asking Yes or No Questions

You can get a *yes* or *no* answer to a question in four ways, discussed in each of the four following sections.

Intonation

Questions are often asked by a noticeable change in **intonation** (modulation of the voice), typified by a rising **inflection** (change in the voice) at the end of the statement. This is the simplest and most colloquial way to ask a question: *Tu veux sortir?* (Do you want to go out?)

To make the question negative, put *ne . . . pas* around the conjugated verb:

■ *Tu ne veux pas sortir?* (Don't you want to go out?)

■ *Tu n'es pas sorti?* (Didn't you go out?)

N'est-ce pas

The tag *n'est-ce pas* has various meanings:

■ isn't that so?

■ right?

■ isn't (doesn't) he/she?

■ aren't (don't) they?

■ aren't (don't) we?

■ aren't (don't) you?

N'est-ce pas is a negative expression, so use *n'est-ce pas* at the end of an affirmative statement: *Tu veux sortir, n'est-ce pas?* (You want to go out, don't you?)

To answer *yes* to a negative question, use *si* instead of *oui*: *Si, je veux sortir.* (Yes, I want to go out.)

Est-ce que

Turn a statement into a question by beginning with the expression *est-ce que*, which is not translated literally, but indicates that a question will follow. This is a common conversational way to ask a question. *Est-ce que tu veux sortir?* (Do you want to go out?)

To make the question negative, place *ne . . . pas* around the conjugated verb:

■ *Est-ce que tu ne veux pas sortir?* (Don't you want to go out?)

■ *Est-ce que tu n'es pas sorti?* (Didn't you go out?)

Inversion

Inversion is the reversal of the word order of the subject pronoun and the conjugated verb in order to form a question: You simply join the verb to its subject pronoun with a hyphen. Inversion is the most formal way to ask a question and is generally used more frequently in writing than in conversation.

The rules for inversion are as follows:

- **Avoid inverting with *je*, which is awkward and rarely used except for the following:**

  ai-je . . . ? (do I have . . . ?)

  suis-je . . . ? (am I . . . ?)

  dois-je . . . ? (must I . . . ?)

  puis-je . . . ? (may I . . . ?[permission])

- **Inversion occurs in all tenses (see Chapters 7, 14, 15, and 16) but only with subject pronouns and conjugated verbs:**

  Sors-tu? (Are you going out?)

  Veux-tu sortir? (Do you want to go out?)

  Es-tu sorti? (Did you go out?)

  Sortais-tu? (Were you going out?)

  Sortirais-tu? (Would you go out?)

  Se lèvent-ils? (Are they getting up?)

  Se sont-ils levés? (Did they get up?)

  The preceding questions can be made negative by putting the first part of the negative phrase before the reflexive pronoun or conjugated verb, and the second part of the negative after the subject pronoun:

  Ne sors-tu jamais? (Don't you ever go out?)

  Ne veux-tu pas sortir? (Don't you want to go out?)

  Ne se sont-ils pas levés? (Didn't they get up?)

- **When the third person singular of the verb *(il, elle, on)* ends in a vowel, a *-t-* is inserted between the verb and the subject pronoun to prevent having two vowels sounds together:**

  Travaille-t-il? (Is he working?)

  A-t-elle fini? (Did she finish?)

But, consider the following:

Obéit-elle? (Does she obey?)

S'est-il lavé? (Did he wash himself?)

■ **With a noun subject, a double-subject construction is used: noun + verb-third person pronoun, for example:** *La fille est-elle sortie?* (Did the girl go out?). The third person pronoun agrees in number and gender with the corresponding subject noun:

Jean est-il blond? (Is John blond?)

Les films sont-ils bons? (Are the films good?)

Cette machine marche-t-elle? (Is that machine working?)

Les filles se sont-elles maquillées? (Did the girls put on makeup?)

Follow the preceding rules to make these sentences negative:

Jean n'est-il pas blond? (Isn't John blond?)

Les films ne sont-ils pas bons? (Aren't the films good?)

Cette machine ne marche-t-elle pas? (Isn't this machine working?)

Les filles ne se sont-elles pas maquillées? (Didn't the girls put on makeup?)

Asking for Information

Use interrogative adjectives, adverbs, and pronouns to ask for information.

Interrogative adjectives

The interrogative adjective *quel* (which?, what?), shown in Table 9-1, agrees in number and gender with the noun it modifies.

Table 9-1   Interrogative Adjectives

Number	*Masculine*	*Feminine*
Singular	*quel*	*quelle*
Plural	*quels*	*quelles*

Quel may be followed by *est-ce que* or inversion:

■ *Quelle chemise est-ce que tu préfères?* (Which shirt do you prefer?)

■ *Quelle chemise préfères-tu?* (Which shirt do you prefer?)

In colloquial French, *quel* + a noun may be placed at the end of the phrase to form the question: *Tu préfères quelle chemise?* (Which shirt do you prefer?)

Quel may also be preceded by a preposition:

■ *De quelle chemise est-ce que tu parles?* (Which shirt are you talking about?)

■ *De quelle chemise parles-tu?* (Which shirt are you talking about?)

Être is the only verb that may separate *quel* from its noun:

■ *Quel est ton nom?* (What's your name?)

■ *Quelle est la date?* (What's the date?)

Interrogative adverbs

The following interrogative adverbs can be used with *est-ce que* or inversion to ask questions.

■ *comment* (how)

■ *combien* (how much/many)

■ *quand* (when)

■ *où* (where)

■ *d'où* (from where)

■ *pourquoi* (why)

In colloquial spoken French, they are often placed after the verb, as follows:

■ *Tu t'appelles comment?* (What's your name?)

■ *Les invités arrivent quand?* (When are the guests arriving?)

With *combien, comment, où, d'où,* and *quand* (but not with *pourquoi*), a question may be formed by inverting a noun subject with a verb that has no object:

- *Où habite cette famille?* (Where does that family live?)

- *Combien coûte ce CD?* (How much does this CD cost?)

Invariable interrogative pronouns

Invariable interrogative pronouns (which do not change), illustrated in Table 9-2, have only one form. No agreement is necessary.

Table 9-2   **Invariable Interrogative Pronouns**

Part of Speech	*People*	*Things*
Subject	who?	what?
	qui	—
	qui est-ce qui	*qu'est-ce qui*
Direct object	whom?	what?
	qui	*que (quoi)*
	qui est-ce que	*qu'est-ce que*
Object of the preposition	who?	what?
	qui	*quoi*
	qui est-ce que	—

Note that the *i* from *qui* is never dropped, whereas *que* becomes *qu'* before a vowel or vowel sound:

Invariable interrogative pronouns are used in the following ways:

- **As subjects, followed by verbs in the third person singular**

    Qui (Qui est-ce qui) est tombé? (Who fell?)

    Qu'est-ce qui est tombé? (What fell?)

    (*Qui* is the short form and *qu'est-ce qui* is the long form. Either is acceptable.)

■ **As objects of the verb**

> *Qui est-ce que tu cherches?* (Whom are you looking for?)
>
> *Qui cherches-tu?* (Whom are you looking for?)
>
> *Tu cherches qui?* (Whom are you looking for?)
>
> *Qu'est-ce que tu cherches?* (What are you looking for?)
>
> *Que cherches-tu?* (What are you looking for?)
>
> *Tu cherches quoi?* (What are you looking for?)

Note that *que* becomes *quoi* after a verb. With *que,* when the subject is a noun, inversion is not performed: *Que cherche Sylvie?* (What is Sylvia looking for?)

■ **As objects of a preposition**

Use a preposition + *qui* for people; use a preposition + *quoi* for things.

> *À qui est-ce que tu parles?* (To whom are you speaking?)
>
> *À qui parles-tu?* (To whom are you speaking?)
>
> *Tu parles à qui?* (To whom are you speaking?)
>
> *De quoi est-ce que tu parles?* (What are you talking about?)
>
> *De quoi parles-tu?* (What are you talking about?)
>
> *Tu parles de quoi?* (What are you talking about?)

À qui shows possession: *À qui est ce livre?* (Whose book is this?)

De qui shows relationship: *De qui es-tu le frère?* (Whose brother are you?)

Variable interrogative pronouns

Variable interrogative pronouns agree in number and gender with the nouns they replace. Select the singular form of the interrogative pronoun to express "which one" and the plural to express "which ones."

■ *Laquelle de ces voitures aimes-tu?* (Which one of these cars do you like?)

■ *Lesquels de ces films as-tu vus?* (Which ones of these films have you seen?)

■ *À laquelle de tes amies écris-tu?* (To which one of your friends are you writing?)

■ *Desquels de ces papiers avez-vous besoin?* (Which ones of these papers do you need?)

Use contractions with the prepositions *à* (to) and *de* (of, from) as shown in Table 9-3:

Table 9-3   Variable Interrogative Pronouns

Number	Masculine	Feminine
Singular	lequel	laquelle
à	auquel	à laquelle
de	duquel	de laquelle
Plural	lesquels	lesquelles
à	auxquels	auxquelles
de	desquels	desquelles

Il y a

Il y a (there is/are or is/are there?) can ask or answer a question, as follows:

■ *Il y a un bal ce soir?* (Is there a party this evening?)

■ *Est-ce qu'il y a un bal ce soir?* (Is there a party this evening?)

■ *Y a-t-il un bal ce soir?* (Is there a party this evening?)

■ *Oui, il y a un bal ce soir.* (Yes, there is a party this evening.)

■ *Il n'y a pas de bal ce soir?* (Isn't there a party this evening?)

■ *Est-ce qu'il n'y a pas de bal ce soir?* (Isn't there a party this evening?)

■ *N'y a-t-il pas de bal ce soir?* (Isn't there a party this evening?)

■ *Non, il n'y a pas de bal ce soir.* (No, there isn't a party this evening.)

Exclaming

Use the adjective *quel* when exclaiming:

■ *Quelle belle histoire!* (What a beautiful story!)

■ *Quelles idées intéressantes!* (What interesting ideas!)

Note that *quel* must agree with the noun it modifies, as shown in Table 9-4.

Table 9-4   Exclamations

Number	Masculine	Feminine
Singular	quel	quelle
Plural	quels	quelles

Chapter Checkout

Select the best word from the list provided to complete the question: *à qui, de qui, qu'est-ce qui, qu'est-ce que, qui est-ce qui, quel, quelle, qui, que, quoi, desquelles, à laquelle, laquelle, combien, comment.*

1. _____ *est ton numéro de téléphone?*

2. _____ *penses-tu de cette idée?*

3. *Tu fais* _____ *ce matin?*

4. _____ *est sur la table?*

5. _____ *de ces écoles vont-ils?*

Answers: 1. *quel* **2.** *que* **3.** *quoi* **4.** *qu'est-ce qui* **5.** *à laquelle*

Chapter 10

ADJECTIVES

Chapter Check-In

❑ Making adjectives agree

❑ Placing adjectives properly

An **adjective** modifies a noun or a pronoun. All French adjectives agree in number (singular or plural) and gender (masculine or feminine) with the nouns they describe. In fact, in French, all words in a sentence must agree with each other: If, for example, the noun or pronoun is singular, its verb and any adjectives describing it must also be singular. If the noun is feminine, the adjective describing it must also be feminine.

Unlike English, most French adjectives are placed after the nouns they modify. A few adjectives, however, precede the noun. In addition, when you use more than one adjective to describe a noun, you must follow placement rules.

Forming Singular Feminine Adjectives from Masculine Adjectives

Most adjectives add *e* to the masculine singular form to get the feminine singular. Be careful when you see masculine adjectives ending in *-e, -eux, -f,* and *-er,* because for those, you do not simply add *e*. (Note that adding this *e* to a previously silent consonant causes that consonant to be pronounced. No pronunication changes occur, however, when adding *e* to a vowel.) See Table 10-1 for a list of common adjectives in their masculine or feminine form.

Table 10-1   Forming Feminine Adjectives

Masculine Singular Adjective	Feminine Singular Adjective
américain (American)	*américaine*
amusant (fun)	*amusante*
bleu (blue)	*bleue*
brun (brunette)	*brune*
blond (blonde)	*blonde*
charmant (charming)	*charmante*
content (happy)	*contente*
court (short)	*courte*
élégant (elegant)	*élégante*
fort (strong)	*forte*
français (French)	*française*
grand (big)	*grande*
haut (tall, big)	*haute*
intelligent (intelligent)	*intelligente*
intéressant (interesting)	*intéressante*
joli (pretty)	*jolie*
lourd (heavy)	*lourde*
ouvert (open)	*ouverte*
parfait (perfect)	*parfaite*
petit (small)	*petite*
poli (polite)	*polie*
prochain (next)	*prochaine*
vrai (true)	*vraie*

Masculine adjectives that end in a silent *e*

Singular adjectives that end in a silent *e* do not change in the feminine. Masculine and feminine forms are spelled and pronounced in the same manner, as follows:

■ *aimable* (kind, pleasant)

■ *célèbre* (famous)

- *comique* (comical)

- *confortable* (comfortable)

- *drôle* (funny)

- *facile* (easy)

- *faible* (weak)

- *formidable* (great)

- *honnête* (honest)

- *magnifique* (magnificent)

- *maigre* (thin)

- *malade* (sick)

- *mince* (thin)

- *moderne* (modern)

- *pauvre* (poor)

- *propre* (clean)

- *sale* (dirty)

- *sincère* (sincere)

- *splendide* (splendid)

- *sympathique* (nice)

- *triste* (sad)

- *vide* (empty)

Masculine adjectives that end in *é*

Form the singular feminine of singular masculine adjectives ending in *é* by adding *-e,* as shown in Table 10-2.

Table 10-2   Forming Feminine Adjectives of Words Ending in *é*

Masculine Singular Adjective	*Feminine Singular Adjective*
âgé (old, aged)	*âgée*
dévoué (devoted)	*dévouée*

Masculine Singular Adjective	Feminine Singular Adjective
fatigué (tired)	fatiguée
occupé (busy)	occupée
situé (situated)	située

Masculine adjectives that end in *eux*

Masculine singular adjectives ending in *eux* form the feminine by changing -x to -se, as shown in Table 10-3.

Table 10-3   Forming Feminine Adjectives of Words Ending in *eux*

Masculine Singular Adjective	Feminine Singular Adjective
affectueux (affectionate)	affectueuse
ambitieux (ambitious)	ambitieuse
chanceux (lucky)	chanceuse
consciencieux (conscientious)	consciencieuse
courageux (courageous)	courageuse
curieux (curious)	curieuse
dangereux (dangerous)	dangereuse
délicieux (delicious)	délicieuse
furieux (furious)	furieuse
généreux (generous)	généreuse
heureux (happy)	heureuse
malheureux (unhappy)	malheureuse
paresseux (lazy)	paresseuse
peureux (fearful)	peureuse
sérieux (serious)	sérieuse

Masculine adjectives that end in *f*

Form the feminine singular of masculine singular adjectives ending in *f* by changing -f to -ve. See Table 10-4.

Table 10-4   Forming Feminine Adjectives of Words Ending in *f*

Masculine Singular Adjective	Feminine Singular Adjective
actif (active)	*active*
attentif (attentive)	*attentive*
imaginatif (imaginative)	*imaginative*
impulsif (impulsive)	*impulsive*
intuitif (intuitive)	*intuitive*
naïf (naive)	*naïve*
neuf (new)	*neuve*
sportif (sporty, athletic)	*sportive*
vif (active)	*vive*

Masculine adjectives that end in *er*

Masculine singular adjectives ending in *-er* form the feminine by changing *-er* to *-ère,* as shown in Table 10-5.

Table 10-5   Forming Feminine Adjectives of Words Ending in *er*

Masculine Singular Adjective	Feminine Singular Adjective
cher (dear, expensive)	*chère*
dernier (last)	*dernière*
entier (entire)	*entière*
étranger (foreign)	*étrangère*
fier (proud)	*fière*
léger (light)	*légère*
premier (first)	*première*

Masculine adjectives that end in consonants

Some masculine singular adjectives form the feminine by doubling the final consonant before the *-e* ending. See Table 10-6.

Table 10-6 Forming Feminine Adjectives of Some Words Ending in Consonants

Masculine Singular Adjective	Feminine Singular Adjective
ancien (ancient, old)	*ancienne*
bas (low)	*basse*
bon (good)	*bonne*
cruel (cruel)	*cruelle*
européen (European)	*européenne*
gentil (nice, kind)	*gentille*
gros (fat, big)	*grosse*

Masculine irregular adjectives

The irregular adjectives shown in Table 10-7 have no rules and must be memorized.

Table 10-7 Irregular Adjectives

Masculine Singular Adjective	Feminine Singular Adjective
beau (beautiful)	*belle*
blanc (white)	*blanche*
complet (complete)	*complète*
doux (sweet, gentle)	*douce*
faux (false)	*fausse*
favori (favorite)	*favorite*
frais (fresh)	*fraîche*
franc (frank)	*franche*
inquiet (worried)	*inquiète*
long (long)	*longue*
nouveau (new)	*nouvelle*
public (public)	*publique*
sec (dry)	*sèche*
secret (secret)	*secrète*
vieux (old)	*vieille*

The French use special forms of *beau (bel), nouveau (nouvel),* and *vieux (vieil)* before masculine nouns beginning with a vowel or vowel sound. If, however, the adjective comes after the noun, the regular masculine form is used:

- *un **bel** arbre* (a beautiful tree); *L'arbre est **beau.*** (The tree is beautiful.)

- *un **nouvel** appartement* (a new apartment); *L'appartement est **nouveau.*** (The apartment is new.)

- *un **vieil** avion* (an old airplane); *L'avion est **vieux.*** (The airplane is old.)

Forming Plural Adjectives from Singular Adjectives

The plural of most adjectives is formed by adding *s* to the singular of the masculine or feminine adjective, as shown in Table 10-8 (feminine form in parentheses).

Table 10-8   Forming Plural Adjectives

Singular Adjective	Plural Adjective
sincère (sincere)	*sincères*
âgé(e) (old)	*âgé(e)s*
fort(e) (strong)	*fort(e)s*
cher(chère) (dear, expensive)	*cher(chère)s*
bon(ne) (good)	*bon(ne)s*
long(ue) (long)	*long(ue)s*

An adjective modifying two or more nouns of different genders uses the masculine plural: *L'homme et sa femme sont généreux.* (The man and his wife are generous.)

Masculine singular adjectives that end in *s* or *x*

If a masculine singular adjective ends in *s* or *x,* the singular and plural are identical, as shown in Table 10-9.

Table 10-9   Forming Plural Adjectives of Words Ending in *s* or *x*

Singular Adjective	Plural Adjective
frais (fresh)	*frais*
bas (low)	*bas*
heureux (happy)	*heureux*

Masculine singular adjectives that end in *al*

For most masculine adjectives ending in *al*, change *-al* to *-aux* in the plural as shown in Table 10-10:

Table 10-10   Forming Plural Adjectives of Words Ending in *al*

Singular Adjective	Plural Adjective
spécial (special)	*spéciaux*
social (social)	*sociaux*
national (national)	*nationaux*

Masculine irregular singular adjectives

Both masculine singular forms of *beau (bel), nouveau (nouvel),* and *vieux (vieil)* have one and the same plural form — see Table 10-11. (Note that *des* becomes *de* before the adjective). See the "Masculine irregular adjectives" section, earlier in this chapter, for a better understanding of using *bel, nouvel,* and *vieil.*

Table 10-11   Forming Irregular Plural Adjectives

Singular Adjective	Plural Adjective
un beau garçon (a handsome boy)	*de beaux garçons*
un bel arbre (a beautiful tree)	*de beaux arbres*
un nouveau livre (a new book)	*de nouveaux livres*
un nouvel hôtel (a new hotel)	*de nouveaux hôtels*
un vieux chapeau (an old hat)	*de vieux chapeaux*
un vieil artiste (an old artist)	*de vieux artistes*

The adjective *tout* (all) is irregular in the masculine plural:

■ **Singular:** *tout*
■ **Plural:** *tous*

Adjective Placement Within Sentences

Most adjectives in French follow the noun they modify, for example, *la maison blanche* (the white house).

A few short, descriptive adjectives, usually expressing beauty, age, goodness, and size (you can remember this with the acronym "BAGS"), generally precede the nouns they modify:

■ **Beauty:** *beau* (beautiful, handsome), *joli* (pretty)
■ **Age:** *nouveau* (new), *vieux* (old), *jeune* (young)
■ **Goodness (or lack of it):** *bon* (good), *gentil* (nice), *mauvais* (bad)
■ **Size:** *grand* (large, big), *petit* (small, little), *court* (short), *long* (long), *gros* (fat)

Other common adjectives that precede the noun but do not fall into the BAGS categories include the following:

■ *autre* (other)
■ *chaque* (each, every)
■ *dernier* (last)
■ *plusieurs* (several)
■ *quelques* (a few)
■ *tel* (such)
■ *tout* (all, whole, every)

Consider the following examples:

■ *un gros livre* (a thick book)
■ *une jolie robe* (a pretty dress)
■ *une autre histoire* (another story)
■ *plusieurs idées* (several ideas)
■ *une telle aventure* (such an adventure)

In addition, *tout* precedes both the noun and the definite article *(le, la, l', les)*.

■ *tous les hommes* (all the men)

■ *toutes les femmes* (all the women)

To use more than one adjective in a description, place each adjective according to whether it precedes or follows the noun. Two adjectives in the same position are joined by *et* (and).

■ *une femme forte et athlétique* (a strong, athletic woman)

■ *un grand et mauvais loup* (a big, bad wolf)

■ *une petite voiture rouge* (a small, red car)

Note that you may use past participles as adjectives, and they must agree with the nouns they modify:

■ *C'était un plaisir inattendu.* (It was an unexpected pleasure.)

■ *Cette table est réservée.* (This table is reserved.)

Chapter Checkout

Put the correct form of the adjective in the correct place:

1. *C'est une fille. (sportif/ambitieux)*
2. *Elle est une femme. (jeune/charmant)*
3. *C'est un artiste. (vieux/sérieux)*
4. *Ils sont deux enfants. (petit/spécial)*
5. *C'est une histoire. (long/intéressant)*

Answers: 1. *C'est une fille sportive et ambitieuse.* **2.** *Elle est une jeune femme charmante.* **3.** *C'est un vieil artiste sérieux.* **4.** *Ils sont deux petits enfants spéciaux.* **5.** *C'est une longue histoire intéressante.*

Chapter 11
ADVERBS

Chapter Check-In

❑ Forming adverbs

❑ Forming adverbial expressions

❑ Placing adverbs properly

An **adverb** is a word that modifies a verb, an adjective, or another adverb. It often expresses how the subject performs an action. In French, many adverbs are formed by adding an ending to the masculine or feminine form of the related adjective (see Chapter 10 for more on adjectives). Other adverbs are totally distinct in nature and must be memorized.

Adverbs in French tend to have the same position in a sentence as they do in English.

Forming Adverbs

Many English adverbs are generally recognized by their "-ly" ending. The equivalent French ending is *-ment*. Unlike the required agreement of French adjectives (discussed in Chapter 10), adverbs in French do not agree with anything because they modify verbs, adjectives, or adverbs and not nouns or pronouns.

To form an adverb, following two rules:

■ **Add *-ment* to the masculine singular form of an adjective that ends with a vowel, as shown in the following table.**

Adjective	Adverb
facile (easy)	*facilement* (easily)
rapide (rapid)	*rapidement* (rapidly)
poli (polite)	*poliment* (politely)
sincère (sincere)	*sincèrement* (sincerely)

■ **If the masculine singular form ends in a consonant, add *-ment* to the feminine singular form of the adjective, as shown in the following table.** Two exceptions include *gentil* (nice), which is *gentille* in its feminine adjective form and *gentiment* (nicely) as an adverb, and *bref* (brief), which is *brève* in its feminine adjective form and *brièvement* (briefly) as an adverb.

Masculine Adjective	Feminine Adjective	Adverb
attentif (attentive)	*attentive*	*attentivement* (attentively)
cruel (cruel)	*cruelle*	*cruellement* (cruelly)
doux (gentle)	*douce*	*doucement* (gently)
entier (entire)	*entière*	*entièrement* (entirely)
faux (false)	*fausse*	*faussement* (falsely)
franc (frank)	*franche*	*franchement* (frankly)
sérieux (serious)	*sérieuse*	*sérieusement* (seriously)
seul (only)	*seule*	*seulement* (only)

Exceptions to the rules for forming adverbs include the following:

■ **For a few adjectives with a silent *-e* ending, remove the ending and add *é* before *-ment*, as shown in the following table.**

Adjective	Adverb
aveugle (blind)	*aveuglément* (blindly)
énorme (enormous)	*énormément* (enormously)
intense (intense)	*intensément* (intensely)

précis (precise)	*précisément* (precisely)
profond (profound)	*profondément* (profoundly)

■ **Adjectives with *-ant* and *-ent* endings have adverbs ending in *-amment* and *-emment*, respectively.** An exception is *lent* (slow), which becomes *lentement* (slowly) in its adverbial form. See the following table for examples.

Adjective	*Adverb*
constant (constant)	*constamment* (constantly)
courant (common)	*couramment* (fluently)
différent (different)	*différemment* (differently)
évident (evident)	*évidemment* (evidently)
récent (recent)	*récemment* (recently)

■ **Some adverbs have forms that are distinct from adjectives and must be memorized.**

Adjective	*Adverb*
bon (good)	*bien* (well)
mauvais (bad)	*mal* (badly)
meilleur (better)	*mieux* (better)
petit (little, small)	*peu* (little)

■ **Some adverbs are not formed from adjectives, as follows:**

alors (then)

après (afterward)

assez (enough)

aujourd'hui (today)

aussi (also, too)

beaucoup (much)

bientôt (soon)

comme (as)

dedans (inside)

dehors (outside)

déjà (already)

demain (tomorrow)

encore (still, yet, again)

enfin (finally, at last)

ensemble (together)

ensuite (then, afterward)

environ (about)

hier (yesterday)

ici (here)

là (there)

loin (far)

longtemps (a long time)

maintenant (now)

même (even)

parfois (sometimes)

partout (everywhere)

peut-être (perhaps, maybe)

plus (more)

près de (near)

presque (almost)

puis (then)

quelquefois (sometimes)

si (so)

souvent (often)

surtout (especially)

tard (late)

tôt (soon, early)

toujours (always, still)

tout (quite, entirely)

très (very)

trop (too much)

vite (quickly)

Adverbial Expressions

Some adverbial expression are formed by combining prepositions with nouns (or noun phrases), adjectives (adjective + a noun), adverbs, or a series of words. Note how this is done in the following examples:

■ **Preposition + noun (noun phrase):** *D'habitude il arrive en retard.* (Generally, he arrives late.)

> *à droite* (to the right)
>
> *à gauche* (to the left)
>
> *à l'heure* (on time)
>
> *à present* (now)
>
> *de temps en temps* (from time to time)
>
> *d'habitude* (generally)
>
> *en retard* (late [in arriving])
>
> *sans doute* (without a doubt)

■ **Preposition + adjective:** *En général elle est très heureuse.* (Generally, she is very happy.)

> *de nouveau* (again)
>
> *d'ordinaire* (ordinarily)
>
> *en général* (generally)

■ **Preposition + adjective + noun:** *Il fait le travail de bon cœur.* (He does the work willingly.)

> *à tout prix* (at any price)
>
> *de bon cœur* (willingly)

de bonne heure (early)

en même temps (at the same time)

■ **Preposition + adverb:** *Il a fait au moins deux erreurs.* (He made at least two mistakes.)

à jamais (forever)

au moins (at least)

du moins (in any case)

■ **Preposition + several words:** *Peu à peu ils font du progrès.* (Little by little, they make progress.)

encore une fois (again)

peu à peu (little by little)

peut-être (perhaps, maybe)

tant pis (too bad)

tout à l'heure (soon)

Certain adverbs used to express quantity are followed by *de* or *d'* (before a vowel). Remember that no article is used before a noun: *Elle a beaucoup d'enfants.* (She has a lot of children.)

■ *assez de* (enough of)

■ *autant de* (as much, many)

■ *beaucoup de* (much, many)

■ *combien de* (how much, many)

■ *moins de* (less, fewer)

■ *peu de* (little, few)

■ *plus de* (more)

■ *tant de* (so much, many)

■ *trop de* (too much, many)

Placing Adverbs Within Sentences

In simple tenses and moods (present, imperfect, future, conditional, subjunctive — see Chapters 7, 15, 16, and 18, respectively), adverbs are generally placed directly after the verbs they modify.

- *Il parle français couramment.* (He speaks French fluently.)
- *Je partirai immédiatement.* (I'll leave immediately.)
- *Vous avez travaillé rapidement.* (You worked quickly.)

Some longer adverbs are placed at the beginning of the sentence: *D'habitude il court très vite.* (Generally, he runs very quickly.) A general rule is to place these longer adverbs in the same position in a French sentence as you would place them in an English sentence.

In the *passé composé* (see Chapter 14), adverbs generally follow the past participle. Some of the more common adverbs — *bien, mal, souvent, toujours, déjà,* and *encore,* and adverbs of quantity — usually precede the past participle, as in the following examples:

- *Il est sorti rapidement.* (He went out quickly.)
- *J'ai déjà vu ce film.* (I already saw that movie.)
- *Elle a acheté beaucoup de livres.* (She bought a lot of books.)

Chapter Checkout

Complete the sentences with an appropriate adverb:

1. *La classe commence à huit heures. Jean arrive à huit heures et demie. Jean arrive _____.*
2. *Michelle fait très attention. Elle écoute _____.*
3. *Luc est un garçon sérieux et il travaille _____.*
4. *M. Rimbaud porte des verres de contact et des lunettes parce qu'il voit _____.*
5. *Il part immédiatement. Ça veut dire qu'il part _____.*

Answers: 1. *en retard* **2.** *attentivement* **3.** *sérieusement* **4.** *mal* **5.** *tout de suite*

Chapter 12
COMPARISONS

Chapter Check-In

❏ Expressing comparisons of inequality

❏ Expressing comparisons of equality

❏ Using comparative and superlative expressions

Comparisons are common in everyday conversations. When making comparisons of inequality, you judge that one thing is more or less superior than another; when making comparisons of equality, you express that both things are equal. Comparisons are made using adjectives, adverbs, and nouns.

Comparative and **superlative** (expressing the extreme degree) expressions allow for **colloquial** (informal) usage of the language. Many of them may be used to express "more" or "less."

Comparisons of Inequality

Comparisons of inequality use adjectives, adverbs, and nouns to show that two things are not equal. In English, comparisons take three forms:

■ **The positive states the fact.**

> Adjective: She is **honest.**

> Adverb: He speaks **fluently.**

> Noun: They do **work.**

■ **The comparative states "more" or "less."** In English, a comparative may end in -er.

> Adjective: I am **taller** than Mary.

> Adverb: He runs **slower** than Tom.

> Noun: I eat **more/less quickly** than Bob.

■ **The superlative states the most or the least — the extreme degree.** In English a superlative may end in -est.

> Adjective: John is the **most/least honest.**

> Adverb: Beth runs the **most/least quickly.**

> Noun: You do the **most/least work** of all.

Positive

The positive states a fact using an adjective, an adverb, or a noun.

■ **Adjective:** *Ma mère est jeune.* (My mother is young.)

■ **Adverb:** *Il parle poliment.* (He speaks politely.)

■ **Noun:** *Je mange des légumes.* (I eat vegetables.)

Comparative

In the comparative, the second element is introduced by *que:*

■ *plus* + adjective (or adverb or noun) + *que* = more . . . than

■ *moins* + adjective (or adverb or noun) + *que* = less . . . than

The second element of the comparative may be a noun (see Chapter 4), a stress pronoun (see Chapter 6), or a **clause** (a group of words). Keep in mind that adjectives must agree in gender and number with the nouns they modify.

■ **Noun:**

> *Ma mère est plus/moins âgée que mon père.* (My mother is older/younger than my father.)

Je mange plus rapidement que mon ami. (I eat more quickly than my friend.)

Je mange plus de légumes que de fruits. (I eat more vegetables than fruits.)

■ **Stress pronoun:**

Ils sont plus intelligents que lui. (They are smarter than he.)

Elle travaille plus sérieusement qu'eux. (She works more seriously than they.)

J'ai plus de travail que toi. (I have more work than you.)

■ **Clause:**

Ce cours est plus facile qu'il croyait. (This course is easier than he believed.)

Tu parles plus couramment que je pensais. (You speak more fluently than I thought.)

Il a plus d'argent qu'il pensait. (He has more money than he thought.)

In addition, when using an adjective to make the comparisons, the second element of the comparison may be an adjective (see Chapter 10): *Elles sont plus énervées que fâchées.* (They are more annoyed than angry.)

Finally, when using either an adjective or an adverb to make the comparison, the second element of the comparison may be an adverb (see Chapter 11):

■ *Elles sont plus fâchées qu'avant.* (They are angrier than before.)

■ *Elle écrit plus vite que correctement.* (She writes more quickly than correctly.)

Superlative
In the superlative, "in" or "of" is expressed by *de* + definite article:

■ *le (la, les) plus* + adjective (or adverb or noun) + *de* = the most . . . in (of)

■ *le (la, les) moins* + adjective (or adverb or noun) + *de* = the least . . . in (of)

Using adjectives

Definite articles and adjectives agree in number and gender with the nouns they modify. If an adjective generally precedes the noun, it retains that position in the superlative:

- *Ma mère est la plus jolie de ses sœurs.* (My mother is the prettiest of her sisters.)

- *Ma mère est la plus jolie sœur.* (My mother is the prettiest sister.)

The adjective may follow the noun, in which case the article is repeated: *Mon père est le frère le plus sage.* (My father is the wisest brother.)

Table 12-1 shows adjectives with irregular comparatives and superlatives:

Table 12-1   Irregular Comparatives and Superlatives—Adjectives

Positive	Comparative	Superlative
bon(ne)(s) (good)	*meilleur(e)(s)* (better)	*le/la/les meilleur(e)(s)* ([the] best)
mauvais(e)(s) (bad)	*plus mauvais(e)(s)* (worse)	*le/la/les plus mauvais(e)(s)* ([the] worst)
	pire(s) (worse)	*le/la/les pire(s)* ([the] worst)

Irregular comparisons and superlatives are used as follows:

- *Tu es ma meilleure amie.* (You are my best friend.)

- *Mon problème est encore pire.* (My problem is even worse.)

Expressions using *bon* require special attention:

- *La table verte est bon marché.* (The green table is cheap.)

- *La table blanche est meilleur marché.* (The white table is cheaper.)

Using adverbs

Adverbs modify verbs so they require no agreement, and *le* is always the article: *Il apprend le plus vite de tout le monde.* (He learns the most quickly of everyone.)

Adverbs with irregular comparatives and superlatives are shown in Table 12-2:

Table 12-2   Irregular Comparatives and Superlatives—Adverbs

Positive	Comparative	Superlative
bien (well)	*mieux* (better)	*le mieux* ([the] best)
mal (badly)	*plus mal* (worse)	*le plus mal* ([the] worst)
mal (badly)	*pis* (worse)	*le pis* ([the] worst)
beaucoup (much)	*plus* (more)	*le plus* ([the] most)
peu (little)	*moins* (less)	*le moins* ([the] least)

The expressions *plus mal* and *le plus mal* are generally preferred to *pis* and *le pis.*

- *Tu parles français mieux que moi.* (You speak French better than I.)
- *Elle se sent plus mal.* (She feels worse.)
- *Je fais le plus de tous les élèves.* (I do the most of all the students.)

Using nouns
Plus and *moins* are adverbs and are, therefore, always preceded by *le,* despite the number and gender of the noun being compared: *Elle chante le plus de toutes les filles.* (She sings the most of all the girls.)

Comparisons of Equality

Comparisons of equality show that two things are the same. The following formula works for adjectives and adverbs: *aussi* + adjective or adverb + *que* (as . . . as):

- *Elle est aussi jolie que sa sœur.* (She is as pretty as her sister.)
- *Il travaille aussi dur que toi.* (He works as hard as you.)

Si usually replaces *aussi* in the negative: *Elles ne sont pas si malheureuse que ça.* (They aren't all that unhappy.)

Use these formulas when the second element is a noun:

- *autant de* + noun + *que* + noun/pronoun (as much/many . . . as)

  Il a autant d'argent que moi. (He has as much money as I.)
- *autant que* + noun/pronoun (as much/many . . . as)

  Elle mange autant que son amie. (She eats as much as her friend.)

Comparative and Superlative Expressions

Use comparative and superlative expressions to speak more idiomatically:

- *faire de son mieux* (to do one's best)

    Je fais de mon mieux. (I do my best.)

- *le plus/moins possible* (as much/little as possible)

    Tu fais le plus/moins possible. (You do the most/least possible.)

- *le plus/le moins . . . possible* (as . . . as possible)

    Je marche le plus/le moins vite possible. (I walk as quickly/slowly as possible.)

- *de plus en plus* (more and more)

    Il devient de plus en plus nerveux. (He becomes more and more nervous.)

- *de moins en moins* (less and less)

    Nous nous inquiétons de moins en moins. (We worry less and less.)

- *de mieux en mieux* (better and better)

    Il lit de mieux en mieux. (He reads better and better.)

- *tant mieux/tant pis* (so much the better/worse)

    Tu pars lundi. (You're leaving Monday.) *Tant mieux.* (So much the better.)

    Il a raté son avion. (He missed his plane.) *Tant pis.* (Too bad.)

Chapter Checkout

Form comparisons by using the clues:

1. *un éléphant/un chien (être + grand)*
2. *un professeur/un dentiste (gagner −)*
3. *les filles/les garçons (être = sportif)*
4. *une comédie/un western (être + amusant)*
5. *un avocat/un docteur (avoir = clients)*

Answers: 1. *Un éléphant est plus grand qu'un chien.* **2.** *Un professeur gagne moins (d'argent) qu'un dentiste.* **3.** *Les filles sont aussi sportives que les garçons.* **4.** *Une comédie est plus amusante qu'un western.* **5.** *Un avocat a autant de clients qu'un docteur.*

Chapter 13
PREPOSITIONS

Chapter Check-In

❑ Using prepositions

❑ Using expressions with prepositions

Prepositions are used to relate elements in a sentence: noun to noun, verb to verb, or verb to noun/pronoun. Prepositions may contract with articles (see Chapter 3).

Prepositions may be used as modifiers and may be used before and after nouns and verbs. Certain verbs are always followed by a preposition. In addition, prepositions are used before the names of geographical locations to refer to travel and location.

Using Prepositions

Prepositions are used to relate two elements of a sentence:

■ Noun to noun: *Il est le fils de M. Legrand.* (He's Mr. Legrand's son.)

■ Verb to verb: *Il commence à pleuvoir.* (It's beginning to rain.)

■ Verb to noun: *Elle travaille avec son ami.* (She works with her friend.)

■ Verb to pronoun: *Elles habitent près de moi.* (They live near me.)

Some prepositions consist of only one word, as follows:

■ *à* (to)

■ *après* (after)

■ *avant* (before)

■ *avec* (with)

- *chez* (at the house of)
- *contre* (against)
- *dans, en* (in)
- *de* (about, from, of)
- *depuis* (since)
- *derrière* (behind)
- *devant* (in front of)
- *entre* (between)
- *malgré* (despite)
- *par* (by, through)
- *parmi* (among)
- *pendant* (during)
- *pour* (for)
- *sans* (without)
- *sauf* (except)
- *selon* (according to)
- *sous* (under)
- *sur* (on)
- *vers* (toward)

Expressing "In"

Three words may be used in French to express "in": *dans, à,* and *en.*

- *Dans* means "inside" or "within an enclosed or specific place" and is often used with an indefinite article *(un, une, des):*

    Mon portefeuille est dans mon sac. (My wallet is inside my purse.)

    Il habite dans une maison. (He lives in a house.)

■ *À* + definite article refers to a general location with no specific boundaries and is usually used with a definite article *(le, la, l', les):*

> *Allons au grand magasin.* (Let's go to the department store.)

■ *En* is used in the following idiomatic expressions: *en ville* (downtown/in the city), *en prison* (in jail):

> *Notre famille dîne en ville.* (Our family is eating in the city.)

The following list shows other prepositions that are formed by using more than one word:

■ *à cause de* (because of)

■ *à côté de* (next to)

■ *à droite* (to the right)

■ *à gauche* (to the left)

■ *à partir de* (beginning with)

■ *à peu près* (nearly)

■ *à propos de* (about, concerning)

■ *à travers* (across, through)

■ *afin de* (in order to)

■ *au (en) bas de* (at the bottom of)

■ *au bout de* (at the end of)

■ *au dessous de* (below, beneath)

■ *au lieu de* (instead of)

■ *au milieu de* (in the middle of)

■ *au sujet de* (about, concerning)

■ *au-dessus de* (above, over)

■ *autour de* (around)

■ *en face de* (opposite)

■ *loin de* (far from)

■ *près de* (near)

Contractions of Two Prepositions

Two prepositions, *à* and *de*, contract with the definite articles *le* and *les* to form new words, as shown in Table 13-1:

Table 13-1   Contractions

Preposition	le	la	l'	les
à	au	à la	à l'	aux
de	du	de la	de l'	des

Contractions are used as follows:

- *Il va au cinéma.* (He goes to the movies.)
- *Il mange des bonbons.* (He eats candy.)

Prepositions with Geographical Locations

Consult Table 13-2 for prepositions that indicate to, from, or in a city, province, country, or continent. Note that most geographical names that end with an *e* are feminine. The exceptions include *le Mexique* (Mexico), *le Cambodge* (Cambodia), and *le Zaïre* (Zaire).

Table 13-2   Prepositions Showing Location

Geographical Location	In	To	From
Cities	à	à	de (d')
Feminine countries, continents, provinces, and islands and masculine countries that begin with a vowel	en	en	de (d')
All other masculine countries	au	au	du
All plurals	aux	aux	des

Prepositional Modifiers

Prepositional modifiers, which describe things, adhere to the following rules:

■ **A preposition + a noun modifying another noun is equivalent to an adjective:**

> *une brosse à cheveux* (a hairbrush)
>
> *une voiture de sport* (a sports car)
>
> *une bague en or* (a gold ring)

■ **The preposition *à* + noun is used to express the use, function, or characteristic of an object or person:**

> *du vernis à ongles* (nail polish)
>
> *une boîte aux lettres* (a mailbox)
>
> *la fille aux yeux bleus* (the girl with blue eyes)

■ **The preposition *à* + verb may be used to describe the purpose of a noun:**

> *une machine à écrire* (a typewriter)

■ **The preposition *de* + noun (and less frequently, *en* + noun) expresses the source or the content of an object:**

> *une robe de soie* (a silk dress)
>
> *des mouchoirs en papier* (tissues)

■ **The preposition *de* + noun combination also expresses possession:**

> *C'est l'ami d'Anne.* (It's Anne's friend.)

■ **A preposition + a noun modifying a verb is equivalent to an adverb:**

> *Ils travaillent avec soin.* (They work carefully.)

Verbs Requiring Indirect Objects

Verbs requiring indirect objects must use a preposition before the object. Although often omitted in English, the preposition is obligatory in French and accompanies the verbs that follow:

■ *appartenir à* (belong to)

■ *apprendre à* (teach)

- *donner à* (give)

- *enseigner à* (teach)

- *obéir à* (obey)

- *pardonner à* (forgive)

- *penser à* (think about)

- *répondre à* (answer)

- *ressembler à* (resemble)

Consider the following examples:

- *Les élèves obéissent au professeur.* (The students obey the teacher.)

- *Les élèves lui obéissent.* (The students obey him.)

Prepositions Before Infinitives

In French, when a verb follows a preposition, the verb is normally in its infinitive form (see Chapter 7). The following sections show verbs requiring *à*, *de*, other prepositions, and *à* + *quelqu'un* + *de*, respectively. The final two sections discuss nouns and adjectives that are followed by *de* before an infinitive and verbs that require no preposition before the infinitive.

Verbs requiring à

The following verbs are followed by the preposition *à*:

- *aider* (help)

- *s'amuser* (have fun)

- *apprendre* (learn to)

- *commencer* (begin)

- *consister* (consist)

- *continuer* (continue)

- *se décider* (decide)

- *encourager* (encourage)

- *enseigner* (teach to)

- *s'habituer* (get used to)

- *se mettre* (begin)
- *persister* (persist)
- *renoncer* (renounce)
- *réussir* (succeed)
- *servir* (serve)
- *songer* (think about)

These verbs are used as follows:

- *Il commence à comprendre.* (He is beginning to understand.)
- *Je réussis à le faire.* (I succeed in doing it.)

Verbs requiring *de*
The following verbs are followed by the preposition *de:*

- *s'arrêter* (stop)
- *décider* (decide)
- *se dépêcher* (hurry)
- *empêcher* (prevent)
- *essayer* (try to)
- *mériter* (deserve)
- *s'occuper* (take care of)
- *oublier* (forget to)
- *parler* (speak about)
- *persuader* (persuade)
- *promettre* (promise)
- *refuser* (refuse)
- *regretter* (regret)
- *rêver* (dream)
- *se souvenir* (remember)
- *venir* (have just)

The preceding verbs are used as follows:

■ *Je m'occuperai de cela.* (I'll take care of that.)

■ *Ils viennent d'arriver.* (They [have] just arrived.)

Verbs requiring other prepositions

The following prepositions are commonly used before the infinitive of a verb:

■ *afin de* (in order to)

■ *au lieu de* (instead of)

■ *avant de* (before)

■ *pour* (for, in order to)

■ *sans* (without)

Note how these prepositions are used in sentences:

■ *Il fait de son mieux afin de réussir.* (He does his best in order to succeed.)

■ *Il dort au lieu de travailler.* (He sleeps instead of working.)

Verbs requiring *à* + *quelqu'un* + *de*

The following verbs require *à quelqu'un de* before an infinitive:

■ *commander* (order)

■ *conseiller* (advise)

■ *défendre* (forbid)

■ *demander* (ask)

■ *dire* (tell)

■ *interdire* (forbid)

■ *ordonner* (order)

■ *permettre* (permit)

■ *promettre* (promise)

Note how the preceding verbs are used:

- *M. Aube défend à son enfant de sortir.* (Mr. Aube forbids his child to leave.)

- *Je lui ai demandé de me téléphoner.* (I asked him to call me.)

Nouns and adjectives followed by *de* before an infinitive

Many nouns and adjectives are followed by *de* before an infinitive:

- *C'est une bonne idée de vous préparer.* (It's a good idea to prepare yourself.)

- *Je suis heureuse de le faire.* (I'm happy to do it.)

Verbs requiring no preposition

The following verbs do not require a preposition before an infinitive that follows:

- *aimer* (like)

- *aimer mieux* (prefer)

- *aller* (go)

- *compter* (intend)

- *désirer* (desire, want)

- *détester* (hate)

- *devoir* (have to)

- *espérer* (hope)

- *falloir* (be necessary)

- *pouvoir* (be able)

- *préférer* (prefer)

- *savoir* (know how)

- *venir* (come)

- *vouloir* (want)

The preceding verbs are used as follows. Note that an adverb may separate the conjugated verb from the infinitive that follows it.

■ *Il sait bien cuisiner.* (He know hows to cook well.)

■ *Je compte revenir.* (I intend to return.)

Chapter Checkout

Fill in a preposition where one is needed:

Une amie est arrivée ___1a___ moi et je l'ai invitée ___1b___ entrer. Elle a passé ___2a___ la porte et s'est assise ___2b___ le sofa. Nous avons parlé ___3___ une dispute que nous avions eue. Elle regrettait ___4___ avoir crié. Je lui ai pardonné ___5___ tout.

Answers: 1a. *chez* **1b.** *à* **2a.** *par* **2b.** *sur* **3.** *d'* **4.** *d'* **5.** *de*

Chapter 14

THE *PASSÉ COMPOSÉ*

Chapter Check-In

❑ Using *avoir* as a helping verb

❑ Using *être* as a helping verb

❑ Using *avoir* or *être* with special verbs

The **compound past tense** (past indefinite), more commonly known as the *passé composé*, refers to an action or event completed in the past. In English, it may be expressed by using the **past participle** (the "-ed" form of the verb) or by using the helping verb "have" or "did" with the past participle: He has finished studying.

The word "compound" in this tense is important because it tells you that this tense is made up of more than one part: Two elements are needed to form the *passé composé*: a **helping verb** (often called an **auxiliary verb**) and a past participle.

Although the overwhelming majority of French verbs use *avoir* (to have) as their helping verb, a few verbs use *être* (to be), and even fewer may use either of these two helping verbs, depending on the meaning the speaker wishes to impart.

The *Passé Composé* with *Avoir*

Using *avoir* as the helping verb is a logical choice in a tense that expresses an action that has occurred. Although English usage often omits the use of "have" when it is implied (you may say, "I lost my keys," and not, "I have lost my keys"), in French, you must always use the helping verb: *J'ai perdu mes clefs.*

To form the *passé composé* of verbs using *avoir*, conjugate *avoir* in the present tense *(j'ai, tu as, il a, nous avons, vous avez, ils ont)* and add the past participle of the verb expressing the action. Put the words together this way: subject + helping verb (usually *avoir*) + past participle.

The *passé composé*, a compound past tense, is formed by combining two elements: when (the action has taken place and, therefore, requires the helping verb *avoir*) and what (the action that has happened and, therefore, requires the past participle of the regular or irregular verb showing the particular action). See Figure 14-1.

Figure 14-1   Forming the *passé composé*.

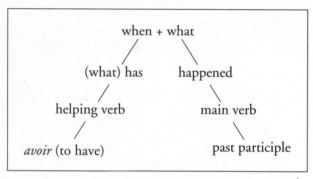

Here are some examples of the *passé composé*.

- *Elle a expliqué son problème.* (She explained her problem.)
- *Ils ont réussi.* (They succeeded.)
- *J'ai entendu les nouvelles.* (I heard the news.)

Forming the negative in the *passé composé* with *avoir*

In a negative sentence in the *passé composé*, *ne* precedes the helping verb, and the negative word (*pas, rien, jamais,* and so on — see Chapter 8) follows it:

- *Je n'ai rien préparé.* (I didn't prepare anything.)
- *Nous n'avons pas fini le travail.* (We didn't finish the work.)
- *Il n'a jamais répondu à la lettre.* (He never answered the letter.)

Questions in the *passé composé* with *avoir*

To form a question in the *passé composé* using inversion, invert the conjugated helping verb with the subject pronoun and add a hyphen. A negative may be placed around the hyphenated helping verb and subject pronoun:

- *As-tu mangé?* (Did you eat?)

- *N'as-tu rien mangé?* (Didn't you eat anything?)

- *A-t-il attendu les autres?* (Did he wait for the others?)

- *N'a-t-il pas attendu?* (Didn't he wait for the others?)

Regular verbs follow a prescribed set of rules for the formation of the past participle, whereas irregular verbs (discussed in the "Past Participles of Irregular Verbs" section) must be memorized. Past participles of verbs conjugated with *avoir* agree in gender (masculine or feminine — add *e*) and number (singular or plural — add *s*) with a preceding direct object noun or pronoun:

- *Le(s) film(s)?* (The film[s]?) *Je l'(les)ai aimé(s).* (I liked it [them].)

- *Quelle(s) robe(s) a-t-elle choisie(s)?* (Which dress[es] did she choose?)

- *Il nous a vus.* (He saw us.)

Past Participles of Regular Verbs

The past participles of regular verbs are formed by dropping the infinitive endings (shown with a line through them), as shown in Table 14-1.

Table 14-1   Regular Past Participles

Verb	-er Verbs	-ir Verbs	-re Verbs
Ending	-é	-i	-u
Infinitive	parler	finir	répondre
Past Participle	parlé	fini	répondu
Example	J'ai parlé à Anne. (I spoke to Ann.)	Nous avons fini. (We have finished.)	Ils ont répondu. (They answered.)

The past participles of shoe verbs (see Chapter 7) require no spelling change within their **stems** (forms to which endings are added):

■ *voyager* (to travel); *Vous avez voyagé.* (You traveled.)

■ *avancer* (to advance); *L'auto a avancé.* (The car advanced.)

■ *payer* (to pay); *Ils ont payé.* (They paid.)

■ *acheter* (to buy); *J'ai acheté un pantalon.* (I bought pants.)

■ *appeler* (to call); *A-t-elle appelé?* (Did she call?)

■ *célébrer* (to celebrate); *Il a célébré son anniversaire.* (He celebrated his birthday.)

Past Participles of Irregular Verbs

In many cases, irregular verbs have irregular past participles and can be grouped according to their endings, as shown in Tables 14-2, 14-3, 14-4, and 14-5.

Table 14-2   Past Participles Ending in -u:

Irregular Verb	Past Participle	English
avoir	eu	had
boire	bu	drank
connaître	connu	known, knew
croire	cru	believed
devoir	dû	had to, owed
lire	lu	read
pleuvoir	plu	rained
pouvoir	pu	was able to
recevoir	reçu	received
savoir	su	knew
voir	vu	seen, saw
vouloir	voulu	wanted

Table 14-3   Past Participles Ending in *-is:*

Irregular Verb	Past Participle	English
mettre	mis	put (on)
prendre	pris	took

Table 14-4   Past Participles Ending in *-it:*

Irregular Verb	Past Participle	English
conduire	conduit	driven, drove
dire	dit	said, told
écrire	écrit	written, wrote

Table 14-5   Other Irregular Past Participles

Irregular Verb	Past Participle	English
être	été	been, was
faire	fait	made, done, did
offrir	offert	offered
ouvrir	ouvert	opened

Irregular verbs that are contained within a larger verb are used as the basis of the past participle:

- *mettre* (put) and *mis* (put); *permettre* (permit) and *permis* (permitted)

- *ouvrir* (open) and *ouvert* (opened); *couvrir* (cover) and *couvert* (covered)

The *Passé Composé* with *Être*

The *passé composé* of 17 verbs is formed by combining the present tense of *être (je suis, tu es, il est, nous sommes, vous êtes, ils sont)* with the past participle of the verb showing the action. Most of these verbs express motion or a change of place, state, or condition (that is, going up, going down, going in, going out, or remaining).

Dr. and Mrs. Vandertrampp live in the house illustrated in Figure 14-2, and defined in Table 14-6. Their name may help you memorize the 17 verbs using *être*. An asterisk (*) denotes an irregular past participle (discussed in the preceding section of this chapter).

Figure 14-2 Verbs using *être* in the *passé composé*.

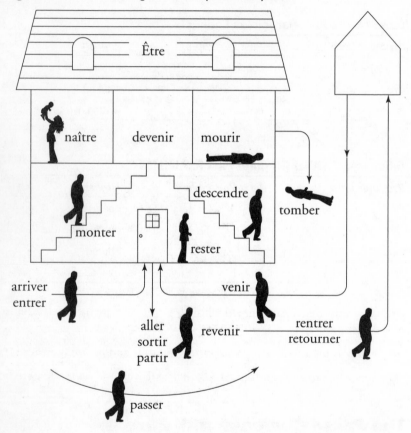

Table 14-6   Verbs Using *Être*

	Verb	Past Participle
D	*devenir* (to become)	*devenu**
R	*revenir* (to come back)	*revenu**
M	*mourir* (to die)	*mort**

	Verb	Past Participle
R	*retourner* (to return)	*retourné*
S	*sortir* (to go out)	*sorti*
V	*venir* (to come)	*venu**
A	*arriver* (to arrive)	*arrivé*
N	*naître* (to be born)	*né**
D	*descendre* (to descend)	*descendu*
E	*entrer* (to enter)	*entré*
R	*rentrer* (to return)	*rentré*
T	*tomber* (to fall)	*tombé*
R	*rester* (to remain)	*resté*
A	*aller* (to go)	*allé*
M	*monter* (to go up)	*monté*
P	*partir* (to leave)	*parti*
P	*passer* (to pass by)	*passé*

Verbs whose helping verb is *être* must show agreement of their past participles in gender (masculine or feminine — add *e*) and number (singular or plural — add *s*) with the subject noun or pronoun, as shown in Table 14-7:

Table 14-7   Agreement with *Être*

Masculine Subjects	Feminine Subjects
je suis allé	*je suis allée*
tu es parti	*tu es partie*
il est venu	*elle est venue*
nous sommes arrivés	*nous sommes arrivées*
vous êtes sorti(s)	*vous êtes sortie(s)*
ils sont morts	*elles sont mortes*

Remember the following rules when using *être* as a helping verb in the *passé composé:*

- *Vous* can be a singular or plural subject for both masculine and feminine subjects.

Singular	*Plural*
Vous êtes entré. (You entered.)	*Vous êtes entrés.* (You entered.)
Vous êtes entrée. (You entered.)	*Vous êtes entrées.* (You entered.)

- For a mixed group, always use the masculine form.

    Roger et Bernard sont revenus. (Roger and Bernard came back.)

    Louise et Mireille sont revenues. (Louise and Mireille came back.)

    Roger et Louise sont revenus. (Roger and Louise came back.)

- If the masculine past participle ends in an unpronounced consonant, pronounce the consonant for the feminine singular and plural forms:

    Il est mort. (He died.) *Ils sont morts.* (They died.)

    Elle est morte. (She died.) *Elles sont mortes.* (They died.)

Forming the negative in the *passé composé* with *être*

In the negative, put *ne* before the conjugated form of *être* and the negative word (see Chapter 8) after it:

- *Il n'est pas sorti.* (He didn't go out.)
- *Elles ne sont pas encore arrivées.* (They didn't arrive yet.)

Questions in the *passé composé* with *être*

To form a question using inversion, invert the conjugated form of *être* with the subject pronoun and add a hyphen. The negatives surround the hyphenated verb and pronoun:

- *Sont-ils partis?* (Did they leave?)
- *Ne sont-ils pas partis?* (Didn't they leave?)

Special Verbs That Use *Être* and *Avoir*

Generally, the verbs *descendre, monter, passer, rentrer, retourner,* and *sortir* use *être* as their helping verb. They may, however, take *avoir* as their helping verb when they are used with a direct object. The meaning of these verbs differs according to the helping verb that is used:

- *descendre:* with *être,* got off, went down; with *avoir,* took down

  Tu es descendu(e) du train. (You got off the train.)

  Je suis descendu(e) l'escalier. (I went downstairs.)

  Il a descendu sa valise. (He took down his suitcase.)

- *monter:* with *être,* went down; with *avoir,* took up

  Elles sont montées. (They went upstairs.)

  Nous avons monté nos affaires. (We took [brought] up our things.)

- *passer:* with *être,* passed by; with *avoir,* spent

  Je suis passé(e) par la pâtisserie. (I passed by the pastry shop.)

  Il a passé un mois au Canada. (He spent a month in Canada.)

- *rentrer:* with *être,* came in; with *avoir,* brought in

  Vous êtes rentré(e)(s) tôt. (You came home early.)

  Elle a rentré le chat. (She brought in the cat.)

- *retourner:* with *être,* returned; with *avoir,* turned over

  Il est retourné à Paris. (He returned to Paris.)

  Ils ont retourné la chaise. (They turned over the chair.)

- *sortir:* with *être,* went out; with *avoir,* took out

  Elles sont sorties. (They went out.)

  Il a sorti son portefeuille. (He took out his wallet.)

Chapter Checkout

Complete the paragraph with the correct form of the *passé composé:*

Pendant l'été, Sylvie (faire)___1___ un voyage à Paris avec sa sœur. Elles (prendre) ___2a___ l'avion. Elles (arriver)___2b___ à l'aéroport Charles de Gaulle où leurs grands-parents les (rencontrer) ___2c___. Ils (aller) ___3___ directement chez eux. Les filles (monter) ___4a___ leurs bagages et puis tout le monde (sortir)___4b___ faire un tour du quartier et ils (manger)___4c___ dans un petit café. Tout d'un coup les filles (devenir)___5a___ très fatiguées et tout le monde (rentrer) ___5b___ à la maison.

Answers: 1. *a fait* **2a.** *ont pris* **2b.** *sont arrivées* **2c.** *ont rencontrées* **3.** *sont allés* **4a.** *ont monté* **4b.** *est sorti* **4c.** *ont mangé* **5a.** *sont devenues* **5b.** *est rentré*

Chapter 15
THE IMPERFECT

Chapter Check-In

❑ Forming and using the imperfect

❑ Comparing the imperfect and the *passé composé*

The **imperfect** is a past tense that has different applications than the *passé composé* (see Chapter 14). In certain circumstances, depending upon the meaning you wish to convey, you have the choice of using either the imperfect or the *passé composé*. Particular words, phrases, and expressions generally indicate which of these two tenses to use in a given circumstance.

The imperfect (or *l'imparfait*) expresses or describes continued, repeated, habitual actual or incomplete actions, situations, or events in the past. In other words, the imperfect describes what was going on at an indefinite time in the past or what used to happen:

■ *Le ciel était bleu.* (The sky was blue.)

■ *L'enfant jouait.* (The child was playing.)

■ *Il chantait toujours.* (He always used to sing.)

The imperfect is unlike the *passé composé* in that it does not use a helping (auxiliary) verb and requires only the addition of specific endings to the **stem** (forms to which endings are added) of the verb. Very few irregularities exist in the imperfect tense.

Regular Verbs

The imperfect is formed by dropping the *-ons* ending of the *nous* form of the present tense of regular verbs (shown with a line through them in Table 15-1) and all irregular verbs except *être*.

Table 15-1   Forming the Imperfect (Examples: *jouer, finir, rendre*)

	je	*tu*	*il, elle*	*nous*	*vous*	*ils, elles*
Nous ending of the present tense				jou~~ons~~ finiss~~ons~~ rend~~ons~~		
Infinitive ending	-ais	-ais	-ait	-ions	-iez	-aient
	jouais	jouais	jouait	jouions	jouiez	jouaient
	finissais	finissais	finissait	finissions	finissiez	finissaient
	rendais	rendais	rendait	rendions	rendiez	rendaient

Verbs already ending in *-ions* in the present tense have an additional *i* before the *-ions* and the *-iez* imperfect endings:

■ *Nous riions.* (We were laughing.)

■ *Vous étudiiez.* (You were studying.)

■ *Nous vérifiions le moteur.* (We were checking the motor.)

To form the negative, place *ne* before the conjugated imperfect form of the verb and place the negative word after it, as follows:

■ *Je ne parlais pas.* (I wasn't speaking.)

■ *Nous ne regardions rien.* (We weren't looking at anything.)

Remember that pronouns remain before the conjugated verb: *Elle ne vous regardait pas.* (She wasn't looking at you.)

Verbs with Spelling Changes

Only two categories of verbs with spelling changes need a closer look in the imperfect:

■ **For verbs ending in *-cer*, change *c* to *ç* before the *a* to keep the soft c (s) sound.** This change occurs only inside the shoe (illustrated in Chapter 7).

j'avançais

tu avançais

il/elle avançait

> *nous avancions*
>
> *vous avanciez*
>
> *ils avançaient*

■ **For verbs ending in *-ger*, insert a silent *e* between *g* and *a* to keep the soft g (zh) sound.** This change occurs only inside the shoe (see Chapter 7).

> *je nageais*
>
> *tu nageais*
>
> *il/elle nageait*
>
> *nous nagions*
>
> *vous nagiez*
>
> *ils nageaient*

Irregular Verbs

Irregular verbs follow the same imperfect formation rules as do regular verbs. Drop the *-ons* from the *nous* form and add the imperfect endings. Consider the following examples:

■ *Tous les ans ils allaient à la plage.* (They used to go to the beach every year.)

■ *Je faisais mes devoirs.* (I was doing my homework.)

The following is a list of the most common irregular present tense verbs whose imperfect forms follow the general rules:

■ *aller* (to go): *nous allons*

■ *avoir* (to have): *nous avons*

■ *boire* (to drink): *nous buvons*

■ *conduire* (to drive): *nous conduisons*

■ *connaître* (to know): *nous connaissons*

■ *croire* (to believe): *nous croyons*

■ *devoir* (to have to): *nous devons*

■ *dire* (to say, tell): *nous disons*

- *dormir* (to sleep): *nous dormons*

- *écrire* (to write): *nous écrivons*

- *faire* (to make, do): *nous faisons*

- *lire* (to read): *nous lisons*

- *mettre* (to put): *nous mettons*

- *offrir* (to offer): *nous offrons*

- *ouvrir* (to open): *nous ouvrons*

- *pouvoir* (to be able to): *nous pouvons*

- *prendre* (to take): *nous prenons*

- *recevoir* (to receive): *nous recevons*

- *savoir* (to know): *nous savons*

- *venir* (to come): *nous venons*

- *voir* (to see): *nous voyons*

- *vouloir* (to wish, want): *nous voulons*

Falloir (to be necessary) and *pleuvoir* (to rain) are used only in the third person singular form in the imperfect: *il fallait* (it was necessary) and *il pleuvait* (it was raining).

The only verb that does not follow the rule for the formation of the imperfect is *être*, which is formed as follows: *j'étais; tu étais; il, elle, on était; nous étions; vous étiez; ils, elles étaient.*

The Imperfect Compared with the *Passé Composé*

The *passé composé* expresses a completed action that occurred at a specific time in the past. This action happened at one moment in time and could have been captured by the click of an instamatic camera.

With that in mind, the following words, phrases, and expressions often require the use of the *passé composé* because they specify a definite past time:

- *l'année passée* (last year)

- *avant-hier* (the day before yesterday)

- *d'abord* (at first)
- *enfin* (finally)
- *ensuite* (then, next)
- *l'été/l'hiver passé* (last summer/winter)
- *finalement* (finally)
- *une fois* (one time)
- *hier* (yesterday)
- *hier soir* (last night)
- *l'autre jour* (the other day)
- *ce jour-là* (that day)
- *un jour* (one day)
- *le mois passé* [*dernier*] (last month)
- *la semaine passée* [*dernière*] (last week)
- *soudain* (suddenly)
- *tout à coup* (suddenly)

The imperfect, on the other hand, expresses an action that continued in the past over an indefinite, undetermined period of time and could have been captured by a video camera. The imperfect also describes what was going on in the past when another action or event took place in the *passé composé: Il sortait quand je suis arrivé(e).* (He was going out when I arrived.)

When "would" means "used to," use the imperfect: *Quand j'étais jeune je lisais beaucoup.* (When I was young, I would read a lot.)

The following expressions generally imply repetitious or habitual past actions and, therefore, require the imperfect:

- *autrefois* (formerly)
- *chaque jour* [*semaine, mois, année*] (each [every] day, week, month, year)
- *de temps à autre* (from time to time)
- *de temps en temps* (from time to time)

- *d'habitude* (usually)
- *d'ordinaire* (usually, generally)
- *en ce temps-là* (at that time)
- *en général* (generally)
- *fréquemment* (frequently)
- *généralement* (generally)
- *habituellement* (habitually)
- *parfois* (sometimes)
- *quelquefois* (sometimes)
- *souvent* (often)
- *toujours* (always)
- *tous les jours* [*mois*] (every day [month])
- *tout le temps* (all the time)

Verbs that indicate a state of mind in the past are generally used in the imperfect.

- *aimer* (to like, love)
- *croire* (to believe)
- *désirer* (to desire)
- *espérer* (to hope)
- *être* (to be)
- *penser* (to think)
- *pouvoir* (to be able to)
- *préférer* (to prefer)
- *regretter* (to regret, be sorry)
- *savoir* (to know [how])
- *vouloir* (to want)

When, however, the state of mind occurred at a specific time in the past, the *passé composé* is used:

- *Je ne pouvais pas l'aider.* (I couldn't help him.)

- *Je n'ai pas pu l'aider hier.* (I couldn't help him yesterday.)

Differences in the use of the *passé composé* and the imperfect are summarized in Table 15-2.

Table 15-2   Comparing the *Passé Composé* and the Imperfect

Passé Composé	*Imperfect*
Expresses specific actions or events that were started and completed at a definite time in the past (even if the time isn't mentioned).	Describes continuous and ongoing actions or events in the past (which may or may not have been completed).
Je suis sorti. (I went out.)	*Il parlait vite.* (He was speaking quickly.)
Expresses a specific action or event that occurred at a specific point in past time.	Describes habitual or repeated actions in the past.
Elle est arrivée hier. (She arrived yesterday.)	*D'habitude il jouait bien.* (Usually, he played well.)
Expresses a specific action or event that was repeated for a stated number of times.	Describes a person, place, thing, or state of mind.
Luc a chanté deux fois. (Luke sang twice.)	*J'étais ravi.* (I was delighted.)

Chapter Checkout

Complete with the correct form of the *passé composé* or the imperfect:

1. *C'est la nuit.* **2.** *Il fait très noir.* **3.** *On ne peut pas voir les étoiles.*
4. *La lune éclaire un peu le ciel.* **5.** *Je dors quand tout d'un coup j'entends quelque chose.*

Answers: 1. *était* **2.** *faisait* **3.** *pouvait* **4.** *éclairait* **5.** *dormais/ai entendu*

Chapter 16

THE FUTURE AND THE CONDITIONAL

Chapter Check-In

❑ Forming and using the future tense

❑ Forming and using the conditional

The **future tense** expresses what the subject will do or is going to do in the future. It also describes what action will or is going to take place at a future time.

The **conditional** is not a tense because it does not refer to a time period. Instead, the conditional is a mood that expresses what a subject would do under certain circumstances.

The future and conditional have the same **stems** (forms to which endings are added), which is why they are grouped together. Their endings and their uses, however, distinguish them one from the other.

Future Tense

Although the future tense is usually used for events taking place in the future, the present tense in French may be used to refer to an action that will take place very soon or to ask for future instructions.

■ *Il part tôt.* (He will be leaving early.)

■ *Je prends le bus?* (Shall I take the bus?)

In addition, you can express an imminent action in the near future by conjugating the verb *aller* (to go) in the present tense and adding the infinitive of the action the speaker will perform, as in the following examples. (Keep in mind that the irregular present tense of aller is *je vais, tu vas, il va, nous allons, vous allez,* and *ils vont.*)

- *Il va aller loin.* (He's going to go far.)

- *Ils vont jouer.* (They are going to play.)

Otherwise, use the future tense in the following cases:

- To express what will happen: *Je réussirai.* (I will succeed.)

- After *quand* (when), *lorsque* (when), *dès que* (as soon as), and *aussitôt que* (as soon as), when referring to a future action, even if the present tense is used in English: *Quand [Lorsque, Dès que, Aussitôt que] nous aurons beaucoup d'argent, nous irons en France.* (When [As soon as] we have a lot of money, we will go to France.)

Future tense of regular verbs

Form the future tense of regular verbs, as shown in Table 16-1, by adding the following endings (often referred to as **avoir endings** because they resemble the present conjugation of avoir) to the verb infinitive. See Chapter 7 for more on regular verbs.

Table 16-1   The Future of Regular Verbs

Subject	Ending	-er Verbs	-ir Verbs	-re Verbs
je	-ai	laverai	punirai	vendrai
tu	-as	laveras	puniras	vendras
il	-a	lavera	punira	vendra
nous	-ons	laverons	punirons	vendrons
vous	-ez	laverez	punirez	vendrez
ils	-ont	laveront	puniront	vendront

Note the following about forming the future tense of regular verbs:

- *-re* verbs drop the final *e* before adding the appropriate future ending: *vendre* (to sell) becomes *nous vendrons* (we will sell)

- The *e* of the *er* infinitive stem of the future is not pronounced.

Future tense and verbs with spelling changes

All verbs that require spelling changes form the future in the same way as regular verbs (see Chapter 7): infinitive + future ending (except the following):

- **For verbs ending in -*yer* (except *envoyer*, which is irregular), change *y* to *i* in all forms of the future tense.** Verbs ending in -*ayer* may or may not make this change:

  j'emploierai, nous emploierons (I will use, we will use)

  je paierai or *je payerai* (I will pay)

- **For verbs ending in *e* + consonant + *er* (but not *é* + consonant + *er*), change the silent *e* before the infinitive ending to *è* in all forms of the future tense.**

  tu achèteras, vous achèterez (you will buy)

- **With *appeler* and *jeter*, double the consonant in the future tense.**

  nous appellerons (we will call)

  nous jetterons (we will throw)

Future tense of irregular verbs

Irregular verbs in the future have future stems ending in -*r* or -*rr*. Add the future endings to these stems to get the correct future form, as shown in Table 16-2.

Table 16-2   Forming the Future Tense with Irregular Verbs

Infinitive	Stem	Examples
aller (to go)	ir-	*J'irai en France.* (I will go to France.)
avoir (to have)	aur-	*Vous aurez un bon voyage.* (You will have a good trip.)
devoir (to have to)	devr-	*Il devra partir bientôt.* (He will have to leave soon.)
être (to be)	ser-	*Nous serons contents.* (We will be happy.)
envoyer (to send)	enverr-	*Elles t'enverront une lettre.* (They will send you a letter.)
faire (to make, do)	fer-	*Tu feras de ton mieux.* (You will do your best.)
pouvoir (to be able to)	pourr-	*Ils pourront sortir ce soir.* (They will be able to go out this evening.)
recevoir (to receive)	recevr-	*Tu recevras une surprise.* (You will receive a surprise.)

Infinitive	Stem	Examples
savoir (to know)	*saur-*	*Il ne saura pas la réponse correcte.* (He will not know the correct answer.)
venir (to come)	*viendr-*	*Je viendrai lundi.* (I will come on Monday.)
voir (to see)	*verr-*	*Nous verrons ce film.* (We will see that film.)
vouloir (to wish, want)	*voudr-*	*Ils voudront vous aider.* (They will want to help you.)

Negating in the future tense

To negate a sentence in the future, simply put *ne* and the negative word (see Chapter 8) around the conjugated verb:

- *Elles ne sortiront pas ce soir.* (They will not go out this evening.)

- *Il ne fumera jamais.* (He will never smoke.)

Remember that pronouns remain before the conjugated verb, as in the following example: *Je ne te téléphonerai pas.* (I will not call you.)

Questions in the future tense

To form a question using inversion, reverse the order of the subject pronoun and the verb and join them with a hyphen:

- *Irez-vous en France cet été?* (Will you go to France this summer?)

- *Jouera-t-elle du piano?* (Will she play the piano.)

The Conditional

Use the conditional in the following situations:

- To express what would happen under certain conditions: *Si j'avais le temps je voyagerais.* (If I had the time, I would travel.)

- When "could" has the sense of "should be able to," in which case you use the conditional of *pouvoir: Il pourrait faire ceci.* (He could [should be able to] do this.)

- To politely make a request or a demand: *Je voudrais l'acheter.* (I would like to buy it.)

The conditional uses the same stem as the future tense, but you then add the conditional endings, which are exactly the same as the imperfect endings (see Chapter 15), as shown in Table 16-3.

Table 16-3   The Conditional of Regular Verbs

Subject	Ending	-er Verbs	-ir Verbs	-re Verbs
je	-ais	laverais	punirais	vendrais
tu	-ais	laverais	punirais	vendrais
il	-ait	laverait	punirait	vendrait
nous	-ions	laverions	punirions	vendrions
vous	-iez	laveriez	puniriez	vendriez
ils	-aient	laveraient	puniraient	vendraient

For irregular verbs and verbs with spelling changes, you simply add conditional endings to the stems used for the future.

- **acheter:** *nous achèterions* (we would buy)
- **aller:** *j'irais* (I would go)
- **appeler:** *vous appelleriez* (you would call)
- **avoir:** *tu aurais* (you would have)
- **devoir:** *il devrait* (he would have to)
- **envoyer:** *j'enverrais* (I would send)
- **essayer:** *j'essaierais* or *j'essayerai* (I would try)
- **être:** *nous serions* (we would be)
- **faire:** *vous feriez* (you would make/do)
- **jeter:** *elle jetterait* (she would throw)
- **pouvoir:** *ils pourraient* (they were able to)
- **recevoir:** *je recevrais* (I would receive)
- **savoir:** *on saurait* (one would know)
- **venir:** *nous viendrions* (we would come)
- **voir:** *vous verriez* (you would see)
- **vouloir:** *ils voudraient* (they would want/wish)

Irregularities in the future and conditional also occur in related verbs:

- *nous mettrions* (we would put); *nous permettrions* (we would permit)
- *j'enverrais* (I would send); *je renverrais* (I would send back)

Negating in the conditional

To negate a sentence in the conditional, simply put *ne* and the negative word (see Chapter 8) around the conjugated verb:

- *Elle ne rirait pas.* (She wouldn't laugh.)
- *Je ne pleurerais pas.* (I wouldn't cry.)

Remember that pronouns remain before the conjugated verb: *Il ne vous punirait pas.* (He wouldn't punish you.)

Questions in the conditional

To form a question using inversion, reverse the order of the subject pronoun and the verb and join them with a hyphen:

- *Voudriez-vous aller en France?* (Would you like to go to France?)
- *Aimerais-tu partir?* (Would you like to leave?)

Chapter Checkout

Complete with the future of the verb:

1. *Dès qu'elle (avoir)_____ le temps, elle vous (envoyer)_____ une lettre.*
2. *Quand nous (aller)_____ en France, nous (acheter)_____ une villa.*
3. *Lorsque je (être)_____ riche, je (faire) _____ le tour du monde.*
4. *Aussitôt que tu (recevoir) _____ le colis, tu (pouvoir) _____ partir.*

Complete with the conditional:

5. *Si nous avions le temps, nous (dormir) _____.*

Answers: 1. *aura/enverra* **2.** *irons/achèterons* **3.** *serai/ferai* **4.** *recevras/pourras* **5.** *dormirions*

Chapter 17

REFLEXIVE VERBS

Chapter Check-In

❑ Conjugating reflexive verbs

❑ Using reflexive verbs with infinitives

❑ Using reflexive verbs in commands

❑ Using reflexive verbs in compound tenses

A **reflexive verb infinitive** is identified by its reflexive pronoun *se,* which is placed before the infinitive (see Chapter 7) and which serves as a direct or indirect object pronoun (see Chapter 6 for more on pronouns). A **reflexive verb** shows that the subject is performing the action upon itself and, therefore, the subject and the reflexive pronoun refer to the same person or thing, as in *je m'appelle* (I call myself), which is translated to "My name is."

Some verbs must always be reflexive, whereas other verbs may be made reflexive by adding the correct object pronoun. The meaning of some verbs varies depending upon whether the verb is used reflexively.

Conjugating Reflexive Verbs

Reflexive verbs are always conjugated with the reflexive pronoun that agrees with the subject: *me* (myself), *te* (yourself), *se* (himself, herself, itself, themselves), *nous* (ourselves), and *vous* (yourself, yourselves). These pronouns generally precede the verb. Follow the rules for conjugating regular verbs, verbs with spelling changes, and irregular verbs (see Chapter 7), as shown in Table 17-1:

Table 17-1   Reflexive Verb Conjugation – Present Tense

Subject	Pronoun	Verb
je	me(m')	lève
tu	te(t')	rases
il/elle/on	se(s')	lave
nous	nous	dépêchons
vous	vous	réveillez
ils/elles	se(s')	couchent

Reflexive constructions have the following meanings.

- **Present tense (see Chapter 7):** *Je me lave.* (I wash myself.)

- *Passé composé* **(see Chapter 14):** *Je me suis lavé(e).* (I washed myself.)

- **Imperfect tense (see Chapter 15):** *Je me lavais.* (I was washing [used to wash] myself.)

- **Future tense (see Chapter 16):** *Je me laverai.* (I will wash myself.)

- **Conditional (see Chapter 16):** *Je me laverais.* (I would wash myself.)

Consider the following most commonly used reflexive verbs. (Those marked with asterisks have shoe verb spelling changes within the infinitive — see Chapter 7 for an illustration of shoe verbs.)

- *s'approcher de* (approach)

- *s'arrêter de* (stop)

- *se baigner* (bathe, swim)

- *se blesser* (hurt oneself)

- *se bronzer* (tan)

- *se brosser* (brush)

- *se brûler* (burn oneself)

- *se casser* (break)

- *se coiffer* (do one's hair)

- *se coucher* (go to bed)

- *se couper* (cut oneself)
- *se demander* (wonder)
- *se dépêcher* (hurry)
- *se déshabiller* (undress)
- *se détendre* (relax)
- *s'endormir* (go to sleep)
- *se fâcher* (become angry)
- *s'habiller* (dress)
- *s'impatienter* (become impatient)
- *s'inquiéter de** (worry about)
- *se laver* (wash)
- *se lever** (get up)
- *se maquiller* (apply makeup)
- *se mettre à* (begin)
- *s'occuper de* (take care of)
- *se peigner* (comb)
- *se présenter* (introduce oneself)
- *se promener** (take a walk)
- *se rappeler** (recall)
- *se raser* (shave)
- *se reposer* (rest)
- *se réunir* (meet)
- *se réveiller* (wake up)
- *se servir de* (use)
- *se tromper* (make a mistake)

In addition, some French verbs are always reflexive despite the fact that in English they are not:

- *s'écrier* (exclaim, cry out)
- *s'en aller* (leave, go away)
- *se fier à* (trust)
- *se méfier de* (distrust)
- *se moquer de* (make fun of)
- *se soucier de* (care about)
- *se souvenir de* (remember)

When a subject is followed by two verbs (and keep in mind that when the first one is conjugated, the second must be in the infinitive — see Chapter 7), the reflexive pronoun generally precedes the infinitive, because its meaning is tied to that verb:

- *Je vais me dépêcher.* (I'm going to hurry.)
- *Il ne va pas se raser.* (He's not going to shave.)

Verbs That Are Both Reflexive and Nonreflexive

The meaning of certain verbs allows the use of the verb either as a reflexive or a nonreflexive verb, depending upon whom the action is performed. *Me, te, se, nous,* and *vous* are also used as direct and indirect object pronouns when not used reflexively. Be sure, therefore, to pay attention to the meaning you wish to convey.

- *Je me lave.* (I wash myself.)
- *Je lave la voiture.* (I wash the car.)
- *Je la lave.* (I wash it.)
- *Il se réveille.* (He wakes [himself] up.)
- *Il me réveille.* (He wakes me up.)

Some verbs in French have different meanings when used reflexively, as shown in Table 17-2.

Table 17-2   Different Meanings for Reflexive Verbs

Basic Meaning	Reflexive Meaning
attendre (wait for)	*s'attendre à* (expect)
battre (beat)	*se battre* (fight)
demander (ask)	*se demander* (wonder)
occuper (occupy)	*s'occuper de* (take care of)
passer (spend time)	*se passer de* (do without)
servir (serve)	*se servir de* (use)
tromper (deceive)	*se tromper* (make a mistake)

Even verbs that are not generally used as reflexive verbs may be made reflexive by adding the reflexive pronoun:

- *Je prépare le dîner.* (I prepare dinner.)

- *Je me prépare.* (I prepare myself.)

Reflexive verbs may be used in the plural to express reciprocal action meaning "each other" or "one another":

- *Nous nous parlons.* (We speak to each other.)

- *Vous vous regardez.* (You look at one another.)

Idiomatic Reflexive Verbs

Finally, some idiomatic reflexive verbs are as follows:

- *se brosser les dents* (brush one's teeth)

- *se casser la jambe* (break one's leg)

- *s'en aller* (go away)

- *se faire des amis* (make friends)

- *se mettre en colère* (get angry)

- *se rendre compte de* (realize)

Consider the following examples:

- *Elle s'en va.* (She's going away.)
- *Il se met en colère.* (He's getting angry.)

Reflexive Verbs and Commands

In a negative command, the reflexive pronoun directly precedes the verb: *Ne te lève pas!* (Don't get up!)

In an affirmative command, the reflexive pronoun follows the verb and is attached to it by a hyphen. In familiar commands, *te* becomes *toi* after the verb: *Lève-toi! Levez-vous!* (Get up!)

Reflexive Verbs and Compound Tenses

In compound tenses like the *passé composé*, reflexive verbs use *être* as their helping (auxiliary) verb — see Chapter 14. The reflexive pronoun remains before the conjugated helping form of *être*, as follows:

- *Je me suis lavé(e).* (I washed myself.)
- *Tu ne t'es pas préparé(e).* (You didn't get ready.)
- *Il s'est rasé.* (He shaved.)
- *Ne s'est-elle pas couchée?* (Didn't she go to bed?)
- *Nous nous sommes peigné(e)s.* (We combed our hair.)
- *Vous ne vous êtes pas coiffé(e)(s).* (You didn't do your hair.)
- *Ils se sont impatientés.* (They became impatient.)
- *Elles se sont maquillées.* (They put on their makeup.)

When the reflexive pronoun is used as a direct object, as in "Whom did they wash? Themselves!," the past participle agrees with the reflexive pronoun that precedes it: *Ils se sont lavés.* (They washed themselves.)

When the reflexive pronoun is used as an indirect object ("To/for whom did they wash something? For themselves!"), the past participle shows no agreement because the direct object comes after the past participle: *Ils se sont lavé la figure.* (They washed their faces.)

Chapter Checkout

Tell what the people do to fix their problems using a reflexive verb:

1. He is late.

2. You (familiar) are unprepared.

3. Your (polite) hair is a mess.

Tell what these people did:

4. Her alarm clock rang.

5. His beard grew too long.

Answers: 1. *Il se dépêche.* **2.** *Tu te prépares.* **3.** *Vous vous peignez.* **4.** *Elle s'est réveillée.* **5.** *Il s'est rasé.*

Chapter 18
THE SUBJUNCTIVE

Chapter Check-In

❑ Forming and using the subjunctive

❑ Avoiding the subjunctive

The **subjunctive** is a mood that reflects the subject's attitude: wishing, wanting, emotions, doubt, denial, and disbelief. Although the subjunctive is used far more frequently in French than in English, you can often avoid using it.

The subjunctive is not a tense (which indicates time) but can be put into a time frame. The **present subjunctive** is the most prevalent and expresses both present and future time.

Uses of the Subjunctive

The present subjunctive refers to actions in the present or the future: *Il est possible que je parte demain.* (It's possible that I will leave tomorrow.)

The subjunctive is needed when all of the following conditions are met:

■ The sentence must contain two different clauses with two different subjects.

■ The clauses must be joined by *que* (that) or, in special instances, by *qui* (who).

■ One of the clauses must show wishing, wanting, need, necessity, emotion, doubt, or denial.

A French sentence using the subjunctive may have a differing English syntax that often omits the word "that" and uses an infinitive instead: *Il est nécessaire que tu arrives tôt.* (You have to arrive early. It is necessary that you arrive early.)

Forms of the Subjunctive

The present subjunctive of regular verbs and of many irregular verbs is formed by dropping the *-ent* from the third person plural *(ils/elles)* form of the present tense (see Chapter 7) and adding the following endings, as shown in Table 18-1:

Table 18-1   The Present Subjunctive of Regular Verbs

Subject	Ending	-er Verbs	-ir Verbs	-re Verbs
		aim**ent**	agiss**ent**	rend**ent**
je	-e	aim**e**	agiss**e**	rend**e**
tu	-es	aim**es**	agiss**es**	rend**es**
il	-e	aim**e**	agiss**e**	rend**e**
nous	-ons	aim**ions**	agiss**ions**	rend**ions**
vous	-ez	aim**iez**	agiss**iez**	rend**iez**
ils	-ent	aim**ent**	agiss**ent**	rend**ent**

Some irregular verbs and some verbs with spelling changes use two different **stems** (the verb forms to which endings are added) to form the present subjunctive, as shown in Table 18-2.

■ The *ils* stem of the present tense for *je, tu, il/elle/on, ils/elles*

■ The *nous* form of the present tense for *nous* and *vous*

Table 18-2   Different Stems for the Present Subjunctive

Verb	Ils Stem	Nous Stem
boire	boiv-	buv-
croire	croi-	croy-
devoir	doiv-	dev-
prendre	prenn-	pren-
recevoir	reçoiv-	recev-
venir	vienn-	ven-
voir	voi-	voy-
manger	mange-	mang-

Verb	Ils Stem	Nous Stem
envoyer	envoi-	envoy-
acheter	achèt-	achet-
appeler	appell-	appel-
préférer	préfèr-	préfér-

Some verbs are completely irregular and must be memorized.

■ *aller: j'aille, tu ailles, il aille, nous allions, vous alliez, il aillent*

■ *avoir: j'aie, tu aies, il ait, nous ayons, vous ayez, ils aient*

■ *être: je sois, tu sois, il soit, nous soyons, vous soyez, ils soient*

■ *faire: je fasse, tu fasses, il fasse, nous fassions, vous fassiez, ils fassent*

■ *pouvoir: je puisse, tu puisses, il puisse, nous puissions, vous puissiez, ils puissent*

■ *savoir: je sache, tu saches, il sache, nous sachions, vous sachiez, ils sachent*

■ *vouloir: je veuille, tu veuilles, il veuille, nous voulions, vous vouliez, ils veuillent*

Remember that the subjunctive form of the verb must be joined to another clause by *que.*

After impersonal expressions

The subjunctive is used in the clause introduced by *que* after impersonal expressions that show opinion, doubt, need, or emotion: *Il est important que vous étudiiez.* (It is important that you study.)

■ *il est absurd* (it is absurd)

■ *il est amusant* (it is amusing)

■ *il est bon* (it is good)

■ *il est curieux* (it is curious)

■ *il est dommage* (it is a pity)

■ *il est douteux* (it is doubtful)

■ *il est essentiel* (it is essential)

- *il est étonnant* (it is amazing)
- *il est étrange* (it is strange)
- *il est gentil* (it is nice)
- *il est impératif* (it is imperative)
- *il est important* (it is important)
- *il est impossible* (it is impossible)
- *il est injuste* (it is unfair)
- *il est intéressant* (it is interesting)
- *il est ironique* (it is ironic)
- *il est juste* (it is fair)
- *il est naturel* (it is natural)
- *il est nécessaire* (it is necessary)
- *il est normal* (it is normal)
- *il est possible* (it is possible)
- *il est préférable* (it is preferable)
- *il est rare* (it is rare)
- *il est regrettable* (it is regrettable)
- *il est surprenant* (it is surprising)
- *il est temps* (it is time)
- *il est urgent* (it is urgent)
- *il est utile* (it is useful)
- *il convient* (it is fitting)
- *il faut* (it is necessary)
- *il semble* (it seems)
- *il suffit* (it is enough)
- *il vaut mieux* (it is better)

For many impersonal expressions, *c'est* may be used in place of *il est: C'est étrange qu'il ne vienne pas.* (It's strange that he isn't coming.)

After verbs and expressions of doubt, denial, and disbelief

The subjunctive is used after verbs and expressions of doubt, denial, and disbelief. The **indicative tenses,** which state facts (present, *passé composé*, imperfect, and future), are used after verbs and expressions of certainty and probability. When these verbs and expressions, shown in Table 18-3, are used in the negative or the interrogative, they imply uncertainty or doubt and require the subjunctive. On the contrary, when doubt is negated, certainty or probability exists and the indicative is used:

- **Subjunctive:** *Il doute que je fasse de mon mieux.* (He doubts that I'll do my best.)

- **Future:** *Il ne doute pas que je ferai de mon mieux.* (He doesn't doubt that I'll do my best.)

Table 18-3   The Subjunctive After Impersonal Expressions

Indicative (Certainty)	Subjunctive (Uncertainty)
je sais (I know)	*je doute* (I doubt)
	je ne sais pas (I don't know)
je suis sûr(e) (I'm sure)	*je ne suis pas sûr(e)* (I'm not sure)
je suis certain(e) (I am certain)	*je ne suis pas certain(e)* (I am not certain)
il est certain (it is certain)	*il n'est pas certain* (it isn't certain)
	il est douteux (it's doubtful)
il est clair (it's clear)	*il n'est pas clair* (it isn't clear)
il est évident (it is evident)	*il n'est pas évident* (it isn't evident)
il est exact (it is exact)	*il n'est pas exact* (it isn't exact)
il paraît (it appears)	*il semble* (it seems)
il est vrai (it's true)	*il n'est pas vrai* (it isn't true)
il est sûr (it is sure)	*il n'est pas sûr* (it isn't sure)
il est probable (it is probable)	*il est possible* (it is possible)
il est improbable (it is improbable)	*il est impossible* (it is impossible)
	il se peut (it is possible)

The subjunctive expresses an action viewed as potential and whose realization is doubted or uncertain. The desired purpose or end may never be met. You can sense a distinct difference in mental outlook between the indicative *il est probable* (it is probable) and the subjunctive *il est possible* (it is possible).

- *Il est probable que tu réussiras.* (It is probable that you will succeed.)
- *Il est possible que tu réussisses.* (It is possible that you will succeed.)

That same difference exists between the indicative *il paraît* (it appears) and the subjunctive *il semble* (it seems).

After verbs of opinion or knowledge, such as *penser* (to think), *croire* (to believe), and *espérer* (to hope), the indicative or the subjunctive is chosen depending upon the meaning of certainty or uncertainty that the speaker wishes to convey. Used affirmatively, these verbs usually require the indicative because they show belief, conviction, or knowledge on the part of the speaker: *Je crois que tu gagneras le match.* (I believe you'll win the match.) Used negatively or interrogatively, these verbs usually (but not always) take the subjunctive because they convey doubt or uncertainty:

- **The speaker has no doubt:** *Crois-tu qu'elle dit la vérité?* (Do you believe she is telling the truth?)
- **The speaker has doubts:** *Crois-tu qu'elle dise la vérité?* (Do you believe she is telling the truth?)

After a wish or a command

The subjunctive is used in the clause following verbs expressing a wish, request, command, permission, prohibition, preference, or desire:

- *aimer mieux* (prefer)
- *commander* (order)
- *conseiller* (advise)
- *consentir* (consent)
- *demander* (ask)
- *défendre* (forbid)
- *désirer* (desire)
- *empêcher* (prevent)
- *exiger* (demand)

- *insister* (insist)
- *ordonner* (order)
- *permettre* (permit)
- *préférer* (prefer)
- *souhaiter* (wish)
- *suggérer* (suggest)
- *vouloir* (want)

Consider the following examples of using the subjunctive after a wish or command:

- *Il préfère que nous restions ici.* (He prefers us to stay here.)
- *Elle insiste que vous fassiez le travail.* (She insists that you do the work.)

After verbs and expressions of emotion and feeling

The subjunctive is used after the following adjectives that express emotion and feeling:

- *content(e)* (content)
- *désolé(e)* (sorry)
- *embarrassé(e)* (embarrassed)
- *ennuyé(e)* (annoyed)
- *enchanté(e), ravi(e)* (delighted)
- *étonné(e)* (astonished)
- *fâché(e)* (angry)
- *fier (fière)* (proud)
- *flatté(e)* (flattered)
- *furieux(euse)* (furious)
- *gêné(e)* (bothered)
- *heureux(euse)* (happy)
- *irrité(e), énervé(e)* (irritated)

- *malheureux(euse)* (unhappy)

- *mécontent(e)* (displeased)

- *surpris(e)* (surprised)

- *triste* (sad)

Do the following to properly use the subjunctive when expressing emotions:

- **Use the subject pronoun + *être* (conjugated) + adjective + *que* + . . . :** *Je suis triste qu'il soit malade.* (I'm sad that he's sick.)

- **Use *avoir* instead of *être* with *peur* (fear) and *honte* (shame):** *Il a honte que vous pleuriez.* (He is ashamed that you are crying.)

After certain conjunctions

Conjunctions are words that connect and relate vocabulary words and pronouns and that connect two clauses in a sentence. They are invariable; that is, their spelling never changes. The subjunctive is used after conjunctions that express the following:

- **Time:** *jusqu'à ce que* (until), *avant que* (before)

  J'attendrai jusqu'à ce qu'il vienne. (I'll wait until he comes.)

- **Purpose:** *pour que* (in order that), *afin que* (so that)

  Je partirai afin qu'il puisse dormir. (I'll leave so that he can sleep.)

- **Concession:** *bien que* (although)

  Il ira bien qu'il soit malade. (He'll go, although he's sick.)

- **Negation:** *sans que* (without)

  Il est arrivé sans qu'elle le sache. (He arrived without her knowing it.)

The following conjunctions take the indicative:

- *après que* (after)

- *aussitôt que* (as soon as)

- *dès que* (as soon as)

- *parce que* (because)

- *pendant que* (while)

- *peut-être que* (perhaps)
- *puisque* (since)
- *tandis que* (while, whereas)

The Subjunctive Versus the Infinitive

If the subjects are exactly the same in meaning in both clauses of a sentence, *que* is omitted and the subjunctive is replaced by the infinitive: *Je voudrais jouer au tennis.* (I want to play tennis.)

However, you say the following: *Je voudrais que nous jouions au tennis.* (I want us to play tennis.)

Chapter Checkout

Complete with the correct verb form:

Georgette est un professeur. En classe il faut qu'elle (mettre) __1__ *ses lunettes et qu'elle (écrire)* __2__ *la leçon au tableau. Il est nécessaire que Georgette (avoir)* __3__ *confiance devant ses élèves. Ils pensent qu'elle (être)* __4__ *très sérieuse parce qu'elle (faire)* __5__ *de grands efforts.*

Answers: 1. *mette* **2.** *écrive* **3.** *ait* **4.** *soit* **5.** *fait*

Appendix A

SYNONYMS AND ANTONYMS

The lists of synonyms and antonyms in Tables A-1 and A-2 give you high-frequency vocabulary words that help you use and understand written and oral French more easily.

Table A-1   Synonyms

Noun	Synonym	English
le chemin	la route	road
l'endroit m.	le lieu	place
la façon	la manière	manner/way
la faute	l'erreur f.	mistake
le médecin	le docteur	docteur
le milieu	le centre	middle/center
les vêtements m.	les habits m.	clothing

Adjective	Synonym	English
certain	sûr	sure
favori	préféré	favorite
grave	sérieux	serious
heureux	content	happy
malheureux	triste	unhappy/sad

Verb	Synonym	English
employer	utiliser	to use
finir	terminer	to finish
habiter	demeurer	to live
préférer	aimer mieux	to prefer
vouloir	désirer	to want

Adverb	Synonym	English
immédiatement	*tout de suite*	immediately
parfois	*quelquefois*	sometimes
puis	*ensuite*	then
rapidement	*vite*	quickly/fast
Preposition	**Synonym**	**English**
entre	*parmi*	among
excepté	*sauf*	except
pendant	*durant*	during

Table A-2   Antonyms

Noun	Antonym
ami/copain m. (friend)	*ennemi m.* (enemy)
le début (beginning)	*la fin* (end)
le jour (day)	*la nuit* (night)
le matin (morning)	*le soir* (evening)
la question (question)	*la réponse* (answer)
la ville (city)	*la campagne* (country)
Adjective	**Antonym**
ancien (old)	*moderne* (modern)
bas (low)	*haut* (high)
beau (beautiful)	*laid* (ugly)
bon (good)	*mauvais* (bad)
chaud (hot)	*froid* (warm)
cher (expensive)	*bon marché* (cheap)
court (short)	*long* (long)
droit (right)	*gauche* (left)
facile (easy)	*difficile* (hard)
fort (strong)	*faible* (weak)

(continued)

Table A-2 *(continued)*

Adjective	Antonym
grand (big)	*petit* (little)
heureux (happy)	*malheureux* (unhappy)
large (wide)	*étroit* (narrow)
léger (light)	*lourd* (heavy)
nouveau (new)	*vieux* (old)
pauvre (poor)	*riche* (rich)
propre (clean)	*sale* (dirty)
vrai (true)	*faux* (false)

Verb	Antonym
accepter (to accept)	*refuser* (to refuse)
acheter (to buy)	*vendre* (to sell)
aimer (to love)	*détester* (to hate)
aller (to go)	*venir* (to come)
arriver (to arrive)	*partir* (to leave)
commencer (to begin)	*finir* (to end)
donner (to give)	*recevoir* (to receive)
emprunter (to borrow)	*prêter* (to lend)
entrer (to enter)	*sortir* (to go out)
fermer (to close)	*ouvrir* (to open)
monter (to go up)	*descendre* (to go down)
perdre (to lose)	*trouver* (to find)
pleurer (to cry)	*rire* (to laugh)
réussir (to succeed)	*râter* (to fail)

Adverb	Antonym
beaucoup (many)	*peu* (few)
bien (well)	*mal* (badly)
ici (here)	*là* (there)
plus (more)	*moins* (less)
vite (quickly)	*lentement* (slowly)

Preposition	Antonym
avant (before)	*après* (after)
avec (with)	*sans* (without)
devant (in front of)	*derrière* (behind)
près (near)	*loin* (far)
sur (on)	*sous* (under)

Appendix B
THEMATIC VOCABULARY

The tables of thematic vocabulary in this appendix give you common, high-frequency words from which to choose when you are looking for a specific word that refers to a particular person, place, or thing.

Table B-1 *La Famille* **(the Family)**

French	English
le cousin	cousin
la cousine	cousin
l'enfant m./f.	child
la femme	wife
la fille	daughter
le fils	son
le frère	brother
la grand-mère	grandmother
le grand-père	grandfather
le mari	husband
la mère	mother
le neveu	nephew
la nièce	niece
l'oncle	uncle
le père	father
la sœur	sister
la tante	aunt

Table B-2   *La Maison* (the House)

French	English
l'appartement m.	apartment
l'ascenseur m.	elevator
le balcon	balcony
la cave	cellar
la chambre	bedroom
la cheminée	fireplace
le couloir	hallway
la cour	courtyard
la cuisine	kitchen
l'escalier m.	stairs
l'étage m.	floor/story
la fenêtre	window
le garage	garage
le grenier	attic
l'immeuble m.	apartment building
le jardin	garden
le mur	wall
la pelouse	lawn
la penderie	clothes closet
la pièce	room
le placard	closet
le plafond	ceiling
le plancher	floor
la porte	door
le rez-de-chaussée	ground floor
la salle à manger	dining room
la salle de bains	bathroom
le salon	living room
le sous-sol	basement

(continued)

Table B-2 *(continued)*

French	English
la terrasse	terrace
le toit	roof

Table B-3 *Les Meubles* (Furniture)

French	English
l'armoire f.	wardrobe
le canapé	sofa
la chaise	chair
la commode	dresser
le congélateur	freezer
la cuisinière	stove
l'étagère f.	bookcase
le fauteuil	armchair
le four	oven
l'horloge f.	clock
le lampadaire	floor lamp
la lampe	lamp
le lave-vaisselle	dishwasher
le lit	bed
la machine à laver	washing machine
le magnétoscope	VCR
le miroir	mirror
le réfrigérateur	refrigerator
le rideau	curtain
le sèche-linge	clothes dryer
la stéréo	stereo
la table	table
le tableau	picture
le tapis	rug
la télévision	television

Table B-4 *Le Quartier* (the Neighborhood)

French	English
l'aéroport m.	airport
l'avenue f.	avenue
la banlieue	suburb
la bibliothèque	library
la bijouterie	jewelry store
la boucherie	butcher shop
la boulangerie	bakery
le boulevard	boulevard
la boutique	shop
le bureau de poste	post office
le centre commercial	mall
le cinéma	movie theater
l'école f.	school
l'édifice m.	building
l'église f.	church
l'épicerie f.	grocery store
le fleuriste	florist
la fruiterie	fruit store
la gare	train station
l'hôpital m.	hospital
la librairie	bookstore
le magasin	store
la mairie	town hall
le musée	museum
le parc	park
la pharmacie	drugstore
la place	square
la rue	street
le stade	stadium

(continued)

Table B-4 *(continued)*

French	English
la station-service	gas station
le supermarché	supermarket
le théâtre	theater
le trottoir	sidewalk

Table B-5 *Les Animaux* (Animals)

French	English
le chat	cat
le cheval	horse
le chien	dog
le cochon	pig
le lapin	rabbit
l'oiseau m.	bird
l'ours m.	bear
la poule	hen
le renard	fox
le singe	monkey
la vache	cow

Table B-6 *Les Repas* (Meals)

French	English
l'addition f.	check
l'assiette f.	plate
la bouteille	bottle
la carte	menu
le couteau	knife
la cuiller/cuillère	spoon
le déjeuner	lunch

French	English
le diner	dinner
la fourchette	fork
la nappe	tablecloth
le petit déjeuner	breakfast
le pourboire	tip
la serviette	napkin
la tasse	cup
le verre	glass

Table B-7 *La Nourriture* **(Food)**

French	English
l'agneau m.	lamb
le beurre	butter
le bifteck	steak
les bonbons m.	candy
le café	coffee
la cerise	cherry
le citron	lemon
la confiture	jam
l'eau minérale f.	mineral water
les épinards m.	spinach
la fraise	strawberry
les frites f.	french fries
le fromage	cheese
le gâteau	cake
la glace	ice cream
les haricots verts m.	green beans
le jambon	ham
le jus	juice

(continued)

Table B-7 *(continued)*

French	English
le lait	milk
les légumes m.	vegetables
l'œuf m.	egg
le pain	bread
la pêche	peach
les petis pois m.	peas
la poire	pear
le poisson	fish
le poivre	pepper
la pomme	apple
la pomme de terre	potato
le poulet	chicken
le raisin	grape
le riz	rice
le sel	salt
le sucre	sugar
le thé	tea
le veau	veal
la viande	meat
le vin	wine

Table B-8 *Le Corps* (the Body)

French	English
la barbe	beard
la bouche	mouth
le bras	arm
les cheveux m.	hair
le cœur	heart
le cou	neck

French	English
le coude	elbow
la dent	tooth
le doigt	finger
le dos	back
l'épaule f.	shoulder
la figure	face
le front	forehead
le genou	knee
la gorge	throat
la jambe	leg
la joue	cheek
la langue	tongue
la lèvre	lip
la main	hand
le menton	chin
le nez	nose
l'œil m.	eye
l'oreille f.	ear
l'orteil m.	toe
la peau	skin
le pied	foot
la poitrine	chest
le sang	blood
la tête	head
le ventre	stomach
le visage	face

Table B-9   *L'Ecole* (School)

French	English
le banc	seat
le bureau	desk
le cahier	notebook
la calculette/calculatrice	calculator
le cartable	briefcase
la carte	map
les ciseaux m.	scissors
le classeur	looseleaf binder
la cloche	bell
le conseiller	counselor
la craie	chalk
le crayon	pencil
les devoirs m.	homework
le dictionnaire	dictionary
le directeur	principal
l'élève m./f.	pupil
l'emploi du temps m.	schedule
l'examen m.	test
la gomme	eraser
la grammaire	grammar
la leçon	lesson
le livre	book
le lycée	high school
le manuel	text
le matériel scolaire	school supplies
le mot	word
la note	grade
le papier	paper

French	English
la phrase	sentence
le professeur	teacher
la règle	ruler
le sac à dos	backpack
le stylo	pen
le tableau	chalkboard
le travail	work
la trousse	pencil case
le vocabulaire	vocabulary

Table B-10 *Les Matières* **(School Subjects)**

French	English
l'anglais m.	English
la chimie	chemistry
le dessin	drawing
l'histoire f.	history
l'informatique f.	computer science
les maths f.	math
la physique	physics

Table B-11 *Les Professions* **(Jobs)**

French	English
l'acteur m.	actor
l'actrice f.	actress
l'agent de police m.	police officer
l'avocat m.	lawyer
le boucher	butcher

(continued)

Table B-11 *(continued)*

French	English
le boulanger	baker
le chercheur	researcher
le coiffeur	hair stylist
le commerçant	merchant
l'écrivain m.	writer
l'épicier m.	grocer
le facteur	mail carrier
le gérant	manager
l'infirmier m.	nurse
l'ingénieur m.	engineer
le juge	judge
le médecin	doctor
l'ouvrier m.	factory worker
le peintre	painter
le programmeur	programmer
le secrétaire	secretary
le vendeur	salesperson

Table B-12 *Les Sports* **(Sports)**

French	English
l'athlétisme m.	track and field
le base-ball	baseball
le football	soccer
la natation	swimming
la pêche	fishing

Table B-13 *Les Couleurs* **(Colors)**

French	English
blanc	white
bleu	blue
brun	brown
gris	gray
jaune	yellow
noir	black
orange	orange
rose	pink
rouge	red
vert	green
violet	purple

Appendix C
VERB CHARTS

The verb charts in this appendix give you all the necessary forms of the present, imperfect, future, conditional, and subjunctive for the most commonly used verbs in French. To express the past tense, select the correct helping verb and add the past participle given for each verb. Use these charts as a quick reference guide when you are searching for the correct form of a regular or high-frequency irregular verb.

Regular Verbs

All regular -er, -ir, and -re verbs follow the same rules in every tense and mood for verb conjugation. Use these sample charts as a guide for all verbs that are classified as regular.

-er verbs

Table C-1   Parler (to speak); Past Participle, parlé

Subject	Present	Imperfect	Future	Conditional	Subjunctive
je	parle	parlais	parlerai	parlerais	parle
tu	parles	parlais	parleras	parlerais	parles
il	parle	parlait	parlera	parlerait	parle
nous	parlons	parlions	parlerons	parlerions	parlions
vous	parlez	parliez	parlerez	parleriez	parliez
ils	parlent	parlaient	parleront	parleraient	parlent

-ir verbs

Table C-2 *Finir* (to finish); Past Participle, *fini*

Subject	Present	Imperfect	Future	Conditional	Subjunctive
je	fin**is**	finiss**ais**	finir**ai**	finir**ais**	finiss**e**
tu	fin**is**	finiss**ais**	finir**as**	finir**ais**	finiss**es**
il	fin**it**	finiss**ait**	finir**a**	finir**ait**	finiss**e**
nous	fin**issons**	finiss**ions**	finir**ons**	finir**ions**	finiss**ions**
vous	fin**issez**	finiss**iez**	finir**ez**	finir**iez**	finiss**iez**
ils	fin**issent**	finiss**aient**	finir**ont**	finir**aient**	finiss**ent**

-re verbs

Table C-3 *Vendre* (to sell); Past Participle, *vendu*

Subject	Present	Imperfect	Future	Conditional	Subjunctive
je	vend**s**	vend**ais**	vendr**ai**	vendr**ais**	vend**e**
tu	vend**s**	vend**ais**	vendr**as**	vendr**ais**	vend**es**
il	vend	vend**ait**	vendr**a**	vendr**ait**	vend**e**
nous	vend**ons**	vend**ions**	vendr**ons**	vendr**ions**	vend**ions**
vous	vend**ez**	vend**iez**	vendr**ez**	vendr**iez**	vend**iez**
ils	vend**ent**	vend**aient**	vendr**ont**	vendr**aient**	vend**ent**

-er verbs with spelling changes
-cer verbs

Table C-4 *Placer* (to place); Past Participle, *placé*

Subject	Present	Imperfect	Future	Conditional	Subjunctive
je	plac**e**	pla**çais**	placer**ai**	placer**ais**	plac**e**
tu	plac**es**	pla**çais**	placer**as**	placer**ais**	plac**es**
il	plac**e**	pla**çait**	placer**a**	placer**ait**	plac**e**
nous	pla**çons**	plac**ions**	placer**ons**	placer**ions**	plac**ions**
vous	plac**ez**	plac**iez**	placer**ez**	placer**iez**	plac**iez**
ils	plac**ent**	pla**çaient**	placer**ont**	placer**aient**	plac**ent**

-ger verbs

Table C-5 *Manger* (to eat); Past Participle, *mangé*

Subject	Present	Imperfect	Future	Conditional	Subjunctive
je	mange	mangeais	mangerai	mangerais	mange
tu	manges	mangeais	mangeras	mangerais	manges
il	mange	mangeait	mangera	mangerait	mange
nous	mangeons	mangions	mangerons	mangerions	mangions
vous	mangez	mangiez	mangerez	mangeriez	mangiez
ils	mangent	mangeaient	mangeront	mangeraient	mangent

-yer verbs

Table C-6 *Employer* (to use); Past Participle, *employé*

Subject	Present	Imperfect	Future	Conditional	Subjunctive
j'	emploie	employais	emploierai	emploierais	emploie
tu	emploies	employais	emploieras	emploierais	emploies
il	emploie	employait	emploiera	emploierait	emploie
nous	employons	employions	emploierons	emploierions	employions
vous	employez	employiez	emploierez	emploieriez	employiez
ils	emploient	employaient	emploieront	emploieraient	emploient

-e + consonant + -er verbs

Table C-7 *Acheter* (to buy); Past Participle, *acheté*

Subject	Present	Imperfect	Future	Conditional	Subjunctive
j'	achète	achetais	achèterai	achèterais	achète
tu	achètes	achetais	achèteras	achèterais	achètes
il	achète	achetait	achètera	achèterait	achète
nous	achetons	achetions	achèterons	achèterions	achetions
vous	achetez	achetiez	achèterez	achèteriez	achetiez
ils	achètent	achetaient	achèteront	achèteraient	achètent

-er verbs with double consonants

Table C-8 *Appeler* (to call); Past Participle, *appelé*

Subject	Present	Imperfect	Future	Conditional	Subjunctive
j'	appelle	appelais	appellerai	appellerais	appelle
tu	appelles	appelais	appelleras	appellerais	appelles
il	appelle	appelait	appellera	appellerait	appelle
nous	appelons	appelions	appellerons	appellerions	appelions
vous	appelez	appeliez	appellerez	appelleriez	appeliez
ils	appellent	appelaient	appelleront	appelleraient	appellent

Table C-9 *Jeter* (to throw); Past Participle, *jeté*

Subject	Present	Imperfect	Future	Conditional	Subjunctive
je	jette	jetais	jetterai	jetterais	jette
tu	jettes	jetais	jetteras	jetterais	jettes
il	jette	jetait	jettera	jetterait	jette
nous	jetons	jetions	jetterons	jetterions	jetions
vous	jetez	jetiez	jetterez	jetteriez	jetiez
ils	jettent	jetaient	jetteront	jetteraient	jettent

-é + consonant + -er verbs

Table C-10 *Répéter* (to repeat); Past Participle, *répété*

Subject	Present	Imperfect	Future	Conditional	Subjunctive
je	répète	répétais	répéterai	répéterais	répète
tu	répètes	répétais	répéteras	répéterais	répètes
il	répète	répétait	répétera	répéterait	répète
nous	répétons	répétions	répéterons	répéterions	répétons
vous	répétez	répétiez	répéterez	répéteriez	répétez
ils	répètent	répétaient	répéteront	répéteraient	répètent

Irregular Verbs

Irregular verbs follow no specific rules for verb conjugation, so you must memorize each one. Use the tables in this section as a reference for the irregular verbs you need the most. (Note that verbs conjugated with *être* in the past tense are indicated by an asterisk [*].)

Table C-11   *Aller** (to go); Past Participle, *allé*

Subject	Present	Imperfect	Future	Conditional	Subjunctive
je	vais	allais	irai	irais	aille
tu	vas	allais	iras	irais	ailles
il	va	allait	ira	irait	aille
nous	allons	allions	irons	irions	allions
vous	allez	alliez	irez	iriez	alliez
ils	vont	allaient	iront	iraient	aillent

Table C-12   *Avoir* (to have); Past Participle, *eu*

Subject	Present	Imperfect	Future	Conditional	Subjunctive
j'	ai	avais	aurai	aurais	aie
tu	as	avais	auras	aurais	aies
il	a	avait	aura	aurait	ait
nous	avons	avions	aurons	aurions	ayons
vous	avez	aviez	aurez	auriez	ayez
ils	ont	avaient	auront	auraient	aient

Table C-13   *Boire* (to drink); Past Participle, *bu*

Subject	Present	Imperfect	Future	Conditional	Subjunctive
je	bois	buvais	boirai	boirais	boive
tu	bois	buvais	boiras	boirais	boives
il	boit	buvait	boira	boirait	boive
nous	buvons	buvions	boirons	boirions	buvions
vous	buvez	buviez	boirez	boiriez	buviez
ils	boivent	buvaient	boiront	boiraient	boivent

Table C-14   *Connaitre* (to know); Past Participle, *connu*

Subject	Present	Imperfect	Future	Conditional	Subjunctive
je	connais	connaissais	connaîtrai	connaîtrais	connaisse
tu	connais	connaissais	connaîtras	connaîtrais	connaisses
il	connaît	connaissait	connaîtra	connaîtrait	connaisse
nous	connaissons	connaissions	connaîtrons	connaîtrions	connaissions
vous	connaissez	connaissiez	connaîtrez	connaîtriez	connaissiez
ils	conaissent	connaissaient	connaîtront	connaîtraient	connaissent

Table C-15   *Devoir* (to have to); Past Participle, *dû*

Subject	Present	Imperfect	Future	Conditional	Subjunctive
je	dois	devais	devrai	devrais	doive
tu	dois	devais	devras	devrais	doives
il	doit	devait	devra	devrait	doive
nous	devons	devions	devrons	devrions	devions
vous	devez	deviez	devrez	devriez	deviez
ils	doivent	devaient	devront	devraient	doivent

Table C-16   *Dire* (to say, tell); Past Participle, *dit*

Subject	Present	Imperfect	Future	Conditional	Subjunctive
je	dis	disais	dirai	dirais	dise
tu	dis	disais	diras	dirais	dises
il	dit	disait	dira	dirait	dise
nous	disons	disions	dirons	dirions	disions
vous	dites	disiez	direz	diriez	disiez
ils	disent	disaient	diront	diraient	disent

Table C-17 *Dormir* (to sleep); Past Participle, *dormi*

Subject	Present	Imperfect	Future	Conditional	Subjunctive
je	dors	dormais	dormirai	dormirais	dorme
tu	dors	dormais	dormiras	dormirais	dormes
il	dort	dormait	dormira	dormirait	dorme
nous	dormons	dormions	dormirons	dormirions	dormions
vous	dormez	dormiez	dormirez	dormiriez	dormiez
ils	dorment	dormaient	dormiront	dormiraient	dorment

Table C-18 *Écrire* (to write); Past Participle, *écrit*

Subject	Present	Imperfect	Future	Conditional	Subjunctive
j'	écris	écrivais	écrirai	écrirais	écrive
tu	écris	écrivais	écriras	écrirais	écrives
il	écrit	écrivait	écrira	écrirait	écrive
nous	écrivons	écrivions	écrirons	écririons	écrivions
vous	écrivez	écriviez	écrirez	écririez	écriviez
ils	écrivent	écrivaient	écriront	écriraient	écrivent

Table C-19 *Être* (to be); Past Participle, *été*

Subject	Present	Imperfect	Future	Conditional	Subjunctive
je	suis	étais	serai	serais	sois
tu	es	étais	seras	serais	sois
il	est	était	sera	serait	soit
nous	sommes	étions	serons	serions	soyons
vous	êtes	étiez	serez	seriez	soyez
ils	sont	étaient	seront	seraient	soient

Table C-20   *Faire* (to make, do); Past Participle, *fait*

Subject	Present	Imperfect	Future	Conditional	Subjunctive
je	fais	faisais	ferai	ferais	fasse
tu	fais	faisais	feras	ferais	fasses
il	fait	faisait	fera	ferait	fasse
nous	faisons	faisions	ferons	ferions	fassions
vous	faites	faisiez	ferez	feriez	fassiez
ils	font	faisaient	feront	feraient	fassent

Table C-21   *Lire* (to read); Past Participle, *lu*

Subject	Present	Imperfect	Future	Conditional	Subjunctive
je	lis	lisais	lirai	lirais	lise
tu	lis	lisais	liras	lirais	lises
il	lit	lisait	lira	lirait	lise
nous	lisons	lisions	lirons	lirions	lisions
vous	lisez	lisiez	lirez	liriez	lisiez
ils	lisent	lisaient	liront	liraient	lisent

Table C-22   *Mettre* (to put); Past Participle, *mis*

Subject	Present	Imperfect	Future	Conditional	Subjunctive
je	mets	mettais	mettrai	mettrais	mette
tu	mets	mettais	mettras	mettrais	mettes
il	met	mettait	mettra	mettrait	mette
nous	mettons	mettions	mettrons	mettrions	mettions
vous	mettez	mettiez	mettrez	mettriez	mettiez
ils	mettent	mettaient	mettront	mettraient	mettent

Table C-23 *Ouvrir* (to open); Past Participle, *ouvert*

Subject	Present	Imperfect	Future	Conditional	Subjunctive
j'	ouvre	ouvrais	ouvrirai	ouvrirais	ouvre
tu	ouvres	ouvrais	ouvriras	ouvrirais	ouvres
il	ouvre	ouvrait	ouvrira	ouvrirait	ouvre
nous	ouvrons	ouvrions	ouvrirons	ouvririons	ouvrions
vous	ouvrez	ouvriez	ouvrirez	ouvririez	ouvriez
ils	ouvrent	ouvraient	ouvriront	ouvriraient	ouvrent

Table C-24 *Partir** (to leave); Past Participle, *parti*

Subject	Present	Imperfect	Future	Conditional	Subjunctive
je	pars	partais	partirai	partirais	parte
tu	pars	partais	partiras	partirais	partes
il	part	partait	partira	partirait	parte
nous	partons	partions	partirons	partirions	partions
vous	partez	partiez	partirez	partiriez	partiez
ils	partent	partaient	partiront	partiraient	partent

Table C-25 *Pouvoir* (to be able to, can); Past Participle, *pu*

Subject	Present	Imperfect	Future	Conditional	Subjunctive
je	peux	pouvais	pourrai	pourrais	puisse
tu	peux	pouvais	pourras	pourrais	puisses
il	peut	pouvait	pourra	pourrait	puisse
nous	pouvons	pouvions	pourrons	pourrions	puissions
vous	pouvez	pouviez	pourrez	pourriez	puissiez
ils	peuvent	pouvaient	pourront	pourraient	puissent

Table C-26   *Prendre* (to take); Past Participle, *pris*

Subject	Present	Imperfect	Future	Conditional	Subjunctive
je	prends	prenais	prendrai	prendrais	prenne
tu	prends	prenais	prendras	prendrais	prennes
il	prend	prenait	prendra	prendrait	prenne
nous	prenons	prenions	prendrons	prendrions	prenions
vous	prenez	preniez	prendrez	prendriez	preniez
ils	prennent	prenaient	prendront	prendraient	prennent

Table C-27   *Recevoir* (to receive); Past Participle, *reçu*

Subject	Present	Imperfect	Future	Conditional	Subjunctive
je	reçois	recevais	recevrai	recevrais	reçoive
tu	reçois	recevais	recevras	recevrais	reçoives
il	reçoit	recevait	recevra	recevrait	reçoive
nous	recevons	recevions	recevrons	recevrions	recevions
vous	recevez	receviez	recevrez	recevriez	receviez
ils	reçoivent	recevaient	recevront	recevraient	reçoivent

Table C-28   *Savoir* (to know); Past Participle, *su*

Subject	Present	Imperfect	Future	Conditional	Subjunctive
je	sais	savais	saurai	saurais	sache
tu	sais	savais	sauras	saurais	saches
il	sait	savait	saura	saurait	sache
nous	savons	savions	saurons	saurions	sachions
vous	savez	saviez	saurez	sauriez	sachiez
ils	savent	savaient	sauront	sauraient	sachent

Table C-29   *Sentir* (to feel, smell); Past Participle, *senti*

Subject	Present	Imperfect	Future	Conditional	Subjunctive
je	sens	sentais	sentirai	sentirais	sente
tu	sens	sentais	sentiras	sentirais	sentes
il	sent	sentait	sentira	sentirait	sente
nous	sentons	sentions	sentirons	sentirions	sentions
vous	sentez	sentiez	sentirez	sentiriez	sentiez
ils	sentent	sentaient	sentiront	sentiraient	sentent

Table C-30   *Servir* (to serve); Past Participle, *servi*

Subject	Present	Imperfect	Future	Conditional	Subjunctive
je	sers	servais	servirai	servirais	serve
tu	sers	servais	serviras	servirais	serves
il	sert	servait	servira	servirait	serve
nous	servons	servions	servirons	servirions	servions
vous	servez	serviez	servirez	serviriez	serviez
ils	servent	servaient	serviront	serviraient	servent

Table C-31   *Sortir** (to go out); Past Participle, *sorti*

Subject	Present	Imperfect	Future	Conditional	Subjunctive
je	sors	sortais	sortirai	sortirais	sorte
tu	sors	sortais	sortiras	sortirais	sortes
il	sort	sortait	sortira	sortirait	sorte
nous	sortons	sortions	sortirons	sortirions	sortions
vous	sortez	sortiez	sortirez	sortiriez	sortiez
ils	sortent	sortaient	sortiront	sortiraient	sortent

Table C-32   *Venir** (to come); Past Participle, *venu*

Subject	Present	Imperfect	Future	Conditional	Subjunctive
je	viens	ven**ais**	viend**rai**	viend**rais**	vienne
tu	viens	ven**ais**	viend**ras**	viend**rais**	viennes
il	vient	ven**ait**	viend**ra**	viend**rait**	vienne
nous	venons	ven**ions**	viend**rons**	viend**rions**	venions
vous	venez	ven**iez**	viend**rez**	viend**riez**	veniez
ils	viennent	ven**aient**	viend**ront**	viend**raient**	viennent

Table C-33   *Voir* (to see); Past Participle, *vu*

Subject	Present	Imperfect	Future	Conditional	Subjunctive
je	vois	voy**ais**	ver**rai**	ver**rais**	voie
tu	vois	voy**ais**	ver**ras**	ver**rais**	voies
il	voit	voy**ait**	ver**ra**	ver**rait**	voie
nous	voyons	voy**ions**	ver**rons**	ver**rions**	voyions
vous	voyez	voy**iez**	ver**rez**	ver**riez**	voyiez
ils	voient	voy**aient**	ver**ront**	ver**raient**	voient

Table C-34   *Vouloir* (to want); Past Participle, *voulu*

Subject	Present	Imperfect	Future	Conditional	Subjunctive
je	veux	voul**ais**	voud**rai**	voud**rais**	veuille
tu	veux	voul**ais**	voud**ras**	voud**rais**	veuilles
il	veut	voul**ait**	voud**ra**	voud**rait**	veuille
nous	voulons	voul**ions**	voud**rons**	voud**rions**	voulions
vous	voulez	voul**iez**	voud**rez**	voud**riez**	vouliez
ils	veulent	voul**aient**	voud**ront**	voud**raient**	veuillent

CQR REVIEW

Use this CQR Review to practice what you've learned in this book. After you work through the review questions, you're well on your way to achieving your goal of mastering French.

Chapter 1

1. _____ and _____ have the same sound.

   a. *On* and *an*
   b. *É* and *er*
   c. *H* and *y*
   d. *Ga* and *gi*

Chapter 2

2. Complete the series: *Lundi, mardi,* _____

   a. *mai*
   b. *mercredi*
   c. *minuit*
   d. *été*

3. Answer the following question: *Quel temps fait-il?* _____

   a. *Il va bien.*
   b. *Il fait un voyage.*
   c. *Il est six heures.*
   d. *Il y a du soleil.*

Chapter 3

4. Complete the sentence: _____ *maison est bleue.*

   a. *La*
   b. *Le*
   c. *L'*
   d. *Les*

5. *Ça* is the abbreviation for _____.

   a. *ceci*
   b. *cette*
   c. *ce*
   d. *cela*

Chapter 4

6. To make the word *fils* plural add _____.

   a. *s*
   b. nothing
   c. *es*
   d. *x*

Chapter 5

7. Complete the sentence: *Jean et Roger adorent* _____ *chien.*

   a. *son*
   b. *ses*
   c. *leur*
   d. *leurs*

Chapter 6

8. Complete the sentence: *Il va au cinéma avec* _____.

   a. *me*
   b. *moi*
   c. *je*
   d. *mon*

Chapter 7

9. To express how you are feeling, use the verb _____.

   a. *aller*
   b. *faire*
   c. *avoir*
   d. *être*

Chapter 8

10. To express "never," use _____.

  a.   *ne . . . que*
  b.   *ne . . . plus*
  c.   *ne . . . jamais*
  d.   *ne . . . rien*

Chapter 9

11. To make an exclamation, use a form of _____.

  a.   *quel*
  b.   *lequel*
  c.   *celui*
  d.   *auquel*

Chapter 10

12. Complete the sentence: *L'hôtel est* _____.

  a.   *vieil*
  b.   *beau*
  c.   *nouvelle*
  d.   *bons*

Chapter 11

13. Complete the sentence: *Elle danse* _____ *que moi.*

  a.   *mieux*
  b.   *meilleur*
  c.   *plus mauvais*
  d.   *peu*

14. A synonym for the adverb *immédiatement* is _____.

  a.   *vite*
  b.   *toujours*
  c.   *parfois*
  d.   *tout de suite*

Chapter 12

15. Complete the sentence: *Je suis plus grande que* _____.

   a. *tu*
   b. *moi*
   c. *il*
   d. *vous*

Chapter 13

16. Complete the sentence: *Nous habitons* _____ *Canada.*

   a. *en*
   b. *au*
   c. *dans*
   d. *de*

Chapters 14 and 15

17. Complete the sentence: *Quand j'étais jeune, je (j')* _____ *l'été en France.*

   a. *passais*
   b. *passe*
   c. *ai passé*
   d. *suis passé*

Chapter 16

18. Complete the sentence: *Hier, à six heures, je (j')* _____ *au restaurant.*

   a. *suis allée*
   b. *allais*
   c. *irai*
   d. *irais*

19. _____ is followed by the present if the future is used in the main clause.

   a. *Quand*
   b. *Dès que*
   c. *Si*
   d. *Lorsque*

Chapter 17

20. Complete the sentence: *Je* _____ *suis couché tard.*

  a. *en*
  b. *la*
  c. *moi*
  d. *me*

Chapter 18

21. Complete the sentence: *Il faut que tu* _____ *immédiatement.*

  a. *viens*
  b. *veuilles*
  c. *viennes*
  d. *voies*

Scenarios (all chapters)

22. You receive a lovely gift from a friend for your birthday. Write a note expressing your thanks and telling how you feel about the gift.

23. You just came back from a trip to France. Write to a relative about your experiences.

Critical Thinking (all chapters)

24. Write a list of what you did over the weekend.

25. Write a list of the things you would do if you won the lottery.

Practice Project (all chapters)

26. Write a dialog between yourself and a person sitting next to you on an airplane. The person is a native French speaker, and you have many questions you would like to have answered. Include your questions and the answers you think the person will give you.

Answers: 1. b **2.** b **3.** d **4.** a **5.** d **6.** b **7.** c **8.** b **9.** a **10.** c **11.** a **12.** b **13.** a **14.** d **15.** d **16.** b **17.** a **18.** a **19.** c **20.** d **21.** c **22.** (sample) *Cher Lucien, Merci beaucoup pour la belle chemise bleue que tu m'as envoyée pour mon anniversaire. Elle est vraiment très jolie et la couleur est parfaite. Tu es vraiment très généreux. Ton ami, Bernard.* **23.** (sample) *Chère Tante Louise, Je viens de rentrer de Paris. J'y ai passé des vacances vraiment excellentes avec des amis. Nous avons visité tous les monuments célèbres. J'ai beaucoup aimé le Louvre et la Tour Eiffel. Notre visite au Centre Georges Pompidou était formidable. Nous nous sommes beaucoup amusés. Je compte te revoir bientôt. J'ai apporté des souvenirs pour toi. Grosses bises, Lisette.*

CQR RESOURCE CENTER

CQR Resource Center offers the best resources available in print and online to help you study and review the core concepts of the French language. You can find additional resources, plus study tips and tools to help test your knowledge, at www.cliffsnotes.com.

Books

This *CliffsQuickReview* book is one of many great books about the study of French. If you want some additional resources, check out these other publications:

Cassell's French Dictionary, by Denis Girard (ed.), Gaston Dulong (ed.), Charles Guinness (ed.), and Oliver Van Oss (ed.), is a hardcover compilation of words, terms, and phrases edited by a team of four renowned linguists. This book also contains French-Canadian usage, including local and regional words and phrases. Hungry Minds, Inc., $24.95.

French For Dummies, complete with CD, by Jean Antonin Billard, Dodin-Katrin Schmidt, Michelle Williams, and Dominique Wenzel, follows the world-famous Berlitz approach to foreign-language acquisition with a fun, user-friendly approach. This book, which contains practical lessons, cultural facts, handy references, verbs lists, and a mini bilingual dictionary, appeals to students and travelers interested in picking up or reviewing basic French. Hungry Minds, Inc., $19.99.

Webster's New World French Dictionary, by Alain Duval and Hélène M.A. Lewis, is a handy, pocket-sized dictionary that is ideal for anyone who needs a French reference book. The book contains up to 90,000 easy-to-read entries with complete coverage of all the words and terms used in standard French, as well as technical jargon and Americanisms. Hungry Minds, Inc., $12.00.

Hungry Minds also has three Web sites that you can visit to read about all the books we publish:

- www.cliffsnotes.com
- www.dummies.com
- www.hungryminds.com

Internet

Visit the following Web sites for more information:

- **French search engines:** Use www.fr.yahoo.com as your search engine to visit French sites. You can learn French by going to French sources.

- **French language:** Visit www.travlang.com, which allows you to listen to and learn basic words and phrases for times, numbers, shopping, travel, directions, and so on. A pronunciation guide is included.

- **French travel:** Go to www.wfi.fr/ to visit a network of sites relating to Paris and France, arranged by categories.

Next time you're on the Internet, don't forget to drop by www.cliffsnotes.com. We created an online Resource Center that you can use today, tomorrow, and beyond.

Newspapers and Magazines

You can find out more about life in France by reading the following:

- *Le monde,* articles from which are available at www.lemonde.fr, is a well-written daily newspaper that prints all of the most important news occurring throughout France.

- Read articles from *Le Figaro,* a popular human-interest newspaper that you can find at www.lefigaro.fr/.

- Go to www.pariscope.fr/ to find out all the latest happenings in and around Paris. This magazine keeps you up-to-date on all events of interest on a weekly basis.

Glossary

accent aigu an accent mark placed over an e (´).

accent circonflexe an accent mark placed over any vowel (^).

accent grave an accent mark placed over an a, e, or u (`).

adjective a word that modifies a noun or a pronoun.

adverb a word that modifies a verb, an adjective, or another adverb.

antecedent a word or group of words to which a relative pronoun refers.

articles small words that are generally classified as adjectives. They indicate that a noun or noun substitute will follow.

auxiliary verb one of two elements needed to form the *passé composé*. Also called a helping verb.

cardinal numbers the numbers we use for counting.

cédille an accent mark placed under a c (¸).

cognates words that are the same or similar in both French and English.

compound past tense see *passé composé*.

conditional mood a mood that expresses what a subject would do under certain circumstances.

conjugation the action of changing the ending of the verb so that it agrees with the subject noun or pronoun performing the task.

definite article translated as "the," it indicates a specific person or thing: the house.

demonstrative adjective an adjective (translated as "this," "that," "these," or "those") that precedes nouns to indicate or point out the person, place, or thing referred to.

direct objects answer the question whom or what the subject is acting upon and may refer to people, places, things, or ideas.

exclamation a word or phrase used to show surprise, delight, incredulity, emphasis, or other strong emotion.

false friends words that are spelled the same or almost the same in both languages but have entirely different meanings and may be different parts of speech.

francophone a French-speaking person.

future tense a tense that expresses what the subject will do or is going to do or what action will or is going to take place at a future time.

gender indicates whether a word is masculine or feminine.

helping verb one of two elements needed to form the *passé composé*. Also called an auxiliary verb.

idiom a particular word or expression whose meaning cannot be readily understood from either its grammar or the words used. Also called an idiomatic expression.

imperfect a past tense that expresses a continuous, repeated, habitual, or incomplete action, situation, or event in the past that was going on at an indefinite time or that used to happen in the past.

indefinite article translated as "a," it refers to persons and objects not specifically identified.

independent (stress) pronouns pronouns used to emphasize a fact or to highlight or replace nouns.

indicative tense a verb tense (present, *passé composé*, imperfect, or future) that states fact.

indirect objects answer the question to or for whom the subject is doing something and refer only to people.

infinitive the basic "to" form of the verb.

intonation the act of asking a question by inserting a rising inflection at the end of a statement.

inversion the reversal of the word order of the subject pronoun and the conjugated verb in order to form a question.

irregular verbs verbs that do not follow a pattern when conjugated.

noun a word used to name a person, place, thing, idea, or quality.

partitive an article asking for an indefinite quantity or part of a whole (translated as "some" or "any").

passé composé a tense that expresses an action or event completed in the past.

past participle the -ed form of a verb.

preposition a word used to relate elements in a sentence: noun to noun, verb to verb, or verb to noun/pronoun.

pronoun a word that is used to replace a noun (a person, place, thing, idea, or quality).

reflexive verb a verb that shows that the subject is performing the action upon itself.

regular verbs verbs that follow a pattern when conjugated.

relative pronoun a pronoun that joins a main clause to a dependent clause (translated as "who," "which," or "that").

shoe verbs verbs with certain spelling changes and irregularities when conjugated.

stem the verb form to which an ending is added.

subject the noun performing the action of the verb.

subjunctive mood a mood expressing wishing, emotion, doubt, or denial.

tréma an accent mark placed over the second of two vowels (¨).

Index

W

Y

Look for These Other Series in the Cliffs Family

Cliffs-QuickReview™

ACT™
Accounting Principles I
Accounting Principles II
Algebra I
Algebra II
American Government
Anatomy and
    Physiology
Astronomy
Basic Math and
    Pre-Algebra
Biochemistry I
Biochemistry II
Biology
Calculus
Chemistry
Criminal Justice
Developmental
    Psychology
Differential Equations
Economics
Geometry
Human Nutrition
Linear Algebra
Microbiology
Organic Chemistry I
Organic Chemistry II
Physical Geology
Physics
Plant Biology
Psychology
SAT® I
Sociology
Statistics
Trigonometry
U.S. History I
U.S. History II

Writing: Grammar,
    Usage, and Style

CliffsTestPrep™

ACT
Advanced Practice for
    the TOEFL® w/2
    cassettes
CBEST®
CLAST
ELM
GMAT CAT®
GRE®
LSAT®
MAT
Math Review for
    Standardized Tests
Memory Power for
    Exams
MSAT
Police Management
    Examinations
Police Officer
    Examination
Police Sergeant
    Examination
Postal Examination
Praxis™ I: PPST
Praxis II: NTE® Core
    Battery
SAT I/PSAT
SAT II Writing
TASP®
TOEFL CBT w/2 CDs
Verbal Review for
    Standardized
    Tests
Writing Proficiency
    Examinations
You Can Pass the GED™

CliffsAP™

AP® Biology
AP Calculus AB
AP Chemistry

AP English Language
    and Composition
AP English Literature
    and Composition
AP United States
    History

Check Out the All-New CliffsNotes Guides

TECHNOLOGY

Balancing Your Check-
    book with Quicken®
Booking Your Next
    Trip Online
Buying and Selling
    on eBay™
Buying Your First PC
Creating a Winning
    PowerPoint® 2000
    Presentation
Creating Web Pages
    with HTML
Creating Your First
    Web Page
Creating Your First
    Web Site with
    FrontPage® 2000
Exploring the World
    with Yahoo!®
Finding What You
    Want on the Web
Getting on the Internet
Getting Started in
    Online Investing
Going Online with
    AOL®
Making Windows®
    Me Millennium
    Edition Work
    for You
Making Windows 98
    Work for You

Setting Up a
    Windows 98
    Home Network
Shopping Online Safely
Taking and Sharing
    Digital Photographs
Upgrading and
    Repairing Your PC
Using Your First iMac™
Using Your First PC
Writing Your First
    Computer Program

PERSONAL FINANCE

Budgeting & Saving
    Your Money
Getting a Loan
Getting Out of Debt
Investing for the
    First Time
Investing in
    401(k) Plans
Investing in IRAs
Investing in
    Mutual Funds
Investing in the
    Stock Market
Managing Your Money
Planning Your
    Retirement
Understanding
    Health Insurance
Understanding
    Life Insurance

CAREERS

Delivering a Winning
    Job Interview
Finding a Job
    on the Web
Getting a Job
Writing a Great Resume

Visit cliffsnotes.com for a complete, updated list of titles

CliffsQuickReview™

Leading educators help you succeed

When it comes to pinpointing the stuff you really need to know, nobody does it better than CliffsNotes. This fast, effective tutorial helps you master French language basics — from pronunciation and accents to the imperfect and the *passé composé* — and get the best possible grade.

At CliffsNotes, we're dedicated to helping you do your best, no matter how challenging the subject. Our authors are veteran teachers and talented writers who know how to cut to the chase — and zero in on the essential information you need to succeed.

Study smarter @ cliffsnotes.com

Free extra review questions
Free info on other resources

Free test-taking tips and tricks
Free CliffsNote-A-Day™ tips

Plus hundreds of downloadable Cliffs titles
24 hours a day

CliffsQuickReviews make studying a snap

CliffsQuickReviews are available for more than 30 introductory level
See inside for a complete listing of these and other bestselling Cliff

ISBN 0-7645-63

$12.99 US
$19.99 CAN
£10.99 UK

Study Aids